The Reflection of the Divine

The Twenty-second Word - The Thirty-second Word - The Thirty-third Word

Bediüzzaman
Said Nursi

Rutherford, New Jersey
2002

Copyright © 2002 by The Light, Inc.
&
Copyright © 2002 by Işık Yayınları

All rights reserved. No part of this book may be reproduced or transmitted in any form or by any means, electronic or mechanical, including photocopying, recording or by any information storage and retrieval system without permission in writing from the Publisher.

Published by The Light, Inc.

42 Park Ave.

Rutherford, NJ 07070 USA

www.thelightinc.com

contact@thelightinc.com

Library of Congress Cataloging-in-Publication
data available

Nursi, Said, 1873-1960.
The Reflection of the Divine /
Bediuzzaman Said Nursi.
p. cm. -- (From the Risale-i nur collection)
Includes index.
ISBN 0-9720654-5-8 (pbk.)

Printed and bound in Turkey

Table of Contents

Bediüzzaman and the Risale-i Nur ii

THE TWENTY-SECOND WORD

Divine Existence and Unity

First station 1

[A parable explaining God's Existence and Unity to an unbeliever through 12 proofs]

Second station 26

[Twelve gleams from the sun of belief in God]

Conclusion 63

THE THIRTY-SECOND WORD

Divine Unity and Oneness •
Human Happiness and Misery

Three Stations 65

[A profound analysis of 21:22 that shows why God needs no partner and why everything glorifies Him with praise]

Supplication 178

THE THIRTY-THIRD WORD

Creation Indicates God's
Existence and Unity

Thirty-three windows 183

[God's necessary Existence and Unity, as well as His Lordship's essential Qualities and Attributes (41:35)]

Index 256

Bediüzzaman and the Risale-i Nur

In the many dimensions of his lifetime of achievement, as well as in his personality and character, Bediüzzaman (1873-1960) was and, through his continuing influence, still is an important thinker and writer in the Muslim world. He represented in a most effective and profound way the intellectual, moral and spiritual strengths of Islam, evident in different degrees throughout its fourteen-century history. He lived for eighty-five years. He spent almost all of those years, overflowing with love and ardor for the cause of Islam, in a wise and measured activism based on sound reasoning and in the shade of the Qur'an and the Prophetic example.

Bediüzzaman lived in an age when materialism was at its peak and many crazed after communism, and the world was in great crisis. In that critical period, Bediüzzaman pointed people to the source of belief and inculcated in them a strong hope for a collective restoration. At a time when science and philosophy were used to mislead young generations into atheism, and nihilistic attitudes had a wide appeal, at a time when all this was done in the name of civilization, modernization and contemporary thinking and those who tried to resist them were subjected to the cruelest of persecutions, Bediüzzaman strove for the overall revival of a whole people, breathing into their minds whatever and spirits whatever is taught in the institutions of both modern and traditional education and of spiritual training.

Bediüzzaman had seen that modern unbelief originated from science and philosophy, not from ignorance as previously. He wrote that nature is the collection of Divine signs and therefore science and religion cannot be conflicting disciplines. Rather, they are two (apparently) different expressions of the same truth. Minds should be enlightened with sciences, while hearts need to be illumined by religion.

Bediüzzaman was not a writer in the usual sense of the word. He wrote his splendid work the *Risale-i Nur*, a collection exceeding 5,000 pages, because he had a mission: he struggled against the materialistic and atheistic trends of thought fed by science and philosophy and tried to present the truths of Islam to modern minds and hearts of every level of understanding. The *Risale-i Nur*, a modern commentary of the Qur'an, mainly concentrates on the existence and unity of God, the Resurrection, Prophethood, the Divine Scriptures primarily including the Qur'an, the invisible realms of existence, Divine Destiny and humanity's free will, worship, justice in human life, and humanity's place and duty among the creation.

In order to remove from people's minds and hearts the accumulated 'sediment' of false beliefs and conceptions and to purify them both intellectually and spiritually, Bediüzzaman writes forcefully and makes reiterations. He writes in neither an academic nor a didactic way; rather he appeals to feelings and aims to pour out his thoughts and ideas into people's hearts and minds in order to awaken them to belief and conviction.

This book is a selected section from the *Risale-i Nur* collection.

The Twenty-second Word

Divine Existence and Unity

In the name of God,
the Merciful, the Compassionate.

First station

Consider the following verses:

> God sets forth parables for humanity in order that they may bear (them) in mind and take lessons (through them). (14:25)

> Such parables do We set forth for humanity so that they may reflect. (59:21)

Once two people[1] washed themselves in a pool and fell into a trance-like state. Upon awakening,

---

[1] The Qur'an declares: *I shall not allow to go to waste the deed of any doer among you, whether male or female. You are one from the other* (3:195). Islam does not discriminate between men and women in religious responsibility. Each gender shares most of the responsibilities, but each one has certain responsibilities that are particular to it. The Qur'an usually uses the masculine form of address, for this is one of

they found themselves in a land of perfect order and harmony. They looked around in amazement: It appeared to them as a vast world, a well-ordered state, a splendid city. If it was looked at from still another point of view, it was a palace that was in itself a magnificent world. They traveled and saw its creatures speaking a language they did not know. However, their gestures indicated that they were doing important work and carrying out significant duties.

One of them said: "This world must have an administrator, this well-ordered state a master, this splendid city an owner, and this skillfully made palace a master builder. We must try to know him, for he brought us here. If we do not, who will help us? What can we expect from those impotent creatures whose language we do not

---

Arabic's characteristics. In almost every language, the masculine form is used for a group comprising both men and women, like the English word *mankind*, which includes both men and women. So, *brotherhood* also includes *sisterhood*, and, since the believers comprise both male and female believers, the believers are bothers and sisters. However, in order to maintain the original text and avoid repetition, usually we do not mention the feminine forms in translation. (Tr.)

know and who ignore us? Moreover, one who has made a huge world in the form of a state, a city, or a palace and filled it with wonderful things, embellished it with every adornment, and decorated it with instructive miracles wants something from us and those who come here. We must know him and learn what he wants."

The other person objected: "There is no such being to govern this world by himself," to which his friend replied: "If we do not recognize him and remain indifferent, we gain nothing and might face some harm. But if we try to recognize him, there is little hardship and the chance of great benefit. So how can we remain indifferent?" The other man insisted: "I find all my ease and enjoyment in not thinking of him. Besides, these things do not concern me. They happened by chance or by themselves." His smart friend replied: "Such obstinacy will get us and many others in trouble. Sometimes a state is ruined because of one ill-mannered person."

The other person turned and said: "Either prove that what you say is true or leave me alone." At that, his friend said: "Since your obstinacy borders on insanity and will cause us to suffer a great calamity, I will show you twelve proofs that this palace-like world, this city-like state, has one master builder who administers it and has no deficiency. He is invisible to us, but must see us and everything and also hear all voices. All his works seem miraculous. All these creatures whom we see but whose languages we do not understand must be his officials [working in his name].

Twelve proofs

FIRST PROOF: Look around. A hidden hand is working in everything, for something without strength is bearing loads weighing thousands of pounds.[2] Something without consciousness is doing much intelligent and purposive work.[3] As they therefore cannot be working on their own, a powerful, hidden one is causing them to work. If everything were happening on its own, all the work being done in this place must itself be a miracle, and everything a miracle-working marvel.

---

[2] This refers to seeds, which bear trees on their heads.

[3] This refers to delicate plants like grapevines, which cannot rise by themselves or bear the weight of fruits, and so throw their delicate arms around other plants or trees and wind themselves around and load themselves onto them.

SECOND PROOF: Look at the adornments of these plains, fields, and residences. Each are marks pointing to that hidden one. Like a seal or stamp, each gives news of him. Look at what he produces from a few grams of cotton.[4] See how many rolls of cloth, linen, and flowered material have come out of it; how much sweet food and other delights are being made.

If thousands of people clothed themselves from these or ate of those, there would still be enough. Again, look. He has taken a handful of iron, soil, water, coal, copper, silver, and gold and made some living creatures.[5] Look and see. These sorts of work are particular to one that holds this land together with all its parts under his miraculous power and all-submissive to his will.

---

[4] For example, an atom-sized poppy seed, an apricot stone that weighs a few grams, or a melon seed each produce from Mercy's treasury woven leaves more beautiful than broadcloth, flowers whiter or yellower than linen, fruits sweeter than sugar, and finer and more delicious than jams, and offer them to us.

[5] This refers to the creation of animal bodies from elements and living creatures from sperm.

THIRD PROOF: Look at these priceless, moving works of art,[6] each fashioned as a miniature specimen of this huge palace. Whatever is in the palace is found in these tiny moving machines. Who but the builder of this amazing palace could include all of it in a tiny machine? Could chance or something purposeless have intervened in this box-sized machine that contains a whole world? However many artistically fashioned machines you see, each is like a seal of that hidden one, like a herald or a proclamation. In their language of being, they say: "We are the works of art of one who can make this entire world as easily as he made us."

FOURTH PROOF: I will show you something even stranger. Look. All things in this land are changing. Each lifeless body and unfeeling "bone" has started to move toward certain purposes, as if each were ruling the others. Look at this machine beside us.[7] It is as though it were issuing com-

---

[6] This refers to animals and human beings. Since an animal is a tiny index of the world, and humanity is a miniature of the universe, whatever is in the universe has a sample that is contained within each human being.

[7] This refers to fruit-bearing trees. As if bearing on their slender branches hundreds of looms and factories, they

mands and all the materials necessary for its adornment and functioning were running to it from distant places. Look over there. That seemingly lifeless body is as though beckoning, for it makes the biggest bodies serve it and work for it.[8] You may compare the rest with these.

Everything seems to have subjugated to itself all creatures in the world. If you do not accept the hidden one's existence, you must attribute all his skills, arts, and perfections to the stones, soil, animals, and creatures resembling people to the things themselves. In place of one miracle-working being, millions of miracle-workers like him have to exist, both opposed to and similar to each other at the same time, and one within the other, without causing any confusion and spoiling the order. But we know that when two rulers intervene in an

---

weave wonderful, richly adorned leaves, blossoms and fruits, and then cook these fruits and offer them to us. Such majestic trees like pines and cedars have set up their workbenches on hard, dry rock to work.

[8] This "body" signifies grains, seeds, and the eggs of flies. A fly leaves its eggs on an elm tree's leaves. Suddenly, the huge tree turns its leaves into a mother's womb, a cradle, a store full of honey-like food, as if it, although not fruit-bearing, produces animate fruit.

affair, the result is confusion. When a village has two headmen, a town two governors, or a country two kings, chaos arises. Given this, what would happen if there were an infinite number of absolute rulers in the same place and at the same time?

FIFTH PROOF: Look carefully at the palace's ornaments and the city's adornments. See this land's orderliness and reflect on this world's artistry. If the pen of a hidden one with infinite miracles and skills is not working, or if all these ornaments are attributed to unconscious causes, blind chance and deaf nature, everything here would have to be a miracle-working decorator and a wonderful inscriber able to write 1,000 books in a letter, and to display infinitely different forms of artistry in a single ornament.

Look at the inscriptions on these stones.[9] Each contains the inscriptions of the whole palace, the laws for the city's order, and the programs for

---

[9] This refers to humanity, the fruit of the Tree of Creation, and to the fruit that bears the program of its tree and its index. Whatever the Pen of Divine Power has inscribed in the great Book of the Universe has been compressed in our creation. Whatever the Pen of Divine Destiny has written in a huge tree has been included in its fingernail-sized fruit.

organizing the state. Given this, making all these inscriptions is as wonderful as making the state. So each inscription and instance of art is a proclamation of that hidden one and one of his seals. A letter indicates its writer, and an artistic inscription makes its inscriber known. Thus how can an inscriber, a designer, or a decorator, who inscribes a huge book in a single letter and displays 1,000 ornaments in a single one, not be known through his inscriptions and ornaments?

SIXTH PROOF: Come onto this vast plain.[10] We will climb to the top of that huge mountain to see the surrounding area. We use these binoculars, for curious things are happening in this land. Every hour things are happening that we never imagined.

Look! These mountains, plains, and towns are suddenly changing so that millions of new things can replace them with perfect orderliness, one

---

[10] This signifies Earth's face in spring and summer, when innumerable individuals of countless species are brought into existence and "written" on Earth. They are recruited and may undergo changes without flaw and with perfect orderliness. Thousands of tables of the Most Merciful One are laid out and then removed and replaced with fresh ones. All trees are like bearers of trays, and all gardens are like cauldrons.

within and after the other. The most curious transformations are occurring. It is as though innumerable kinds of cloths are being woven inside and among others. Familiar flowery things are being replaced in an orderly fashion with others of similar nature but different form. Everything is happening as if each plain and mountain is a page upon which infinite different books are being written without flaw or defect. It is inconceivable that these things, which display infinite art, skill, and exactness, come about on their own. Rather, they show the artist who engenders them. The one who does all these things displays such miracles, for nothing is difficult for him. It is as easy for him to write 1,000 books as to write one book.

Look around. He puts everything in its proper place with such wisdom, pours his favor so generously on the needy and deserving, draws back and opens general veils and doors so bountifully that all are satisfied, and lays out such munificent tables that a feast of bounties is given to all of this land's people and animals. Indeed, the bounties are particular and suitable for each group and individual. How can this be attributed to chance, be purposeless or vain, or have many hands behind it? The only reasonable explanation is that their maker is powerful over everything, that everything is subjugated to him. So, my friend, what pretext can you find to persist in your denial?

SEVENTH PROOF: Let's turn to the mutual interrelations of this amazing palace-like world's parts. Universal things are being done and general revolutions are taking place with such perfect orderliness that all rocks, soil, and trees in this palace obey this world's general rules as if each were free to do whatever it wills. Things that are most distant come to each other's aid. Look at that strange caravan coming from the unseen on mounts resembling trees, plants, and mountains.[11] Each member is carrying trays of food on its head and bringing it to the animals waiting on this side. Look at the mighty electric lamp in that dome.[12] It not only provides light, but also cooks their food so well that the food to be cooked is attached to a string by an unseen hand and held out and offered.[13] See these impotent, weak, defenseless little animals.

---

[11] "Caravans" of plants and trees bearing the sustenance of all animals.

[12] An allusion to the sun.

[13] The string and its attached food denote a tree's slender branches and the delicious fruits thereon.

Over their heads are small, spring-like "pumps" full of delicate sustenance.[14] They only have to press their mouths against these pumps to be fed.

In short, all things in this world, as if positioned face-to-face, help each other. As though seeing each other, they cooperate with each other. To perfect each other's work, they support each other and work together. Their ways of cooperation cannot be counted. All of this proves that everything is subjugated to the builder of that wonderful palace, the real owner of this world. Everything works on his behalf, like a soldier carrying out his commands. Everything takes place by his power, moves by his command, and is arranged through his wisdom. Everything helps the others by his munificence, and everything is made to hasten to the aid of others through his compassion. O my friend, can you object to this?

EIGHTH PROOF: Come, O my friend who supposes yourself to be intelligent, as does my own selfhood. You do not want to recognize this magnificent palace's owner although everything points to him, shows him, and testifies to him.

---

[14] The breasts of mothers.

How can you deny such testimony? Given this, you have to deny the palace as well and say: "There is no world, no state." Deny your own existence, too, and disappear, or else come to your senses and listen to me.

In the palace are uniform elements and minerals that encompass the whole land.[15] Everything is made from them. This means that whoever owns them owns everything made from them, for whoever owns the field owns its crops, and whoever owns the sea owns its contents. These textiles and decorated woven clothes are made from a single substance. Obviously, the one who creates the substance both prepares it and makes it into yarn, for such a work does not allow the participation of others. Therefore, all of the things skillfully woven out of it are particular to him.

All types of such woven things are found throughout the land. They are being made all

---

[15] Elements and minerals denote the elements of air, water, light, and soil, which perform numerous systematic duties: By Divine permission, they hasten to help all needy beings, enter everywhere by Divine command and provide help, convey the necessities of life, and "suckle" living creatures. They also function as the source, origin, and cradle for the weaving and decoration of Divine artifacts.

together, one inside or among others, in the same way and at the same instant. They can be the work only of one person who does everything with one command. Otherwise such correspondence and conformity as regards time, fashion, and quality would be impossible. So, each skillfully made thing is proclaims that hidden one and points to him. It is as if each kind of flowered cloth, skillfully made machine, and delicious morsel is a stamp, a seal, a sign of that miracle-working one.

It is also as if each is saying in the language of its being: "Whoever owns me as a work of art also owns the boxes and shops in which I am found." Each decoration says: "Whoever embroidered me also wove the roll of cloth in which I am located." Each delicious morsel says: "Whoever cooked me also has the cooking pot in which I am located." Each machine says: "Whoever made me also makes all those like me that are found throughout the land. The one who raises us everywhere is also the same. As this same person owns the land and this palace, he also must own us."

This is because the real owner of, say a cartridge-belt or a button belonging to the state, has to own the factories in which they are made. If someone ignorantly claims ownership of it, it will be taken away. Such people will be punished for pretending to own the state's property.

In short, if each element has permeated through every other and encompasses the whole, their owner only can be the one who owns all the land. Since the instances of art found everywhere resemble each other and display the same stamp, whatever has spread throughout the land is evidently the work of a single person's art. And, that one rules over everything. Thus there is a sign of oneness, a stamp of unity in this magnificent palace-like land. Some things are uniform, unique, and of the same nature, yet all-encompassing. Other things, though various and abundant, display a unity of grouping since they resemble each other and are found everywhere. Such unity declares the one of unity. That means that this land's builder, host, and owner must be one and the same.

Look attentively. See how a thickish string[16] has appeared from behind the veil of the Unseen.

---

[16] The "thick string" is a fruit-bearing tree, the strings are its branches, and the diamond decorations, favors, and gifts are the various flowers and fruits hung thereon.

See how thousands of strings hang down from it. See their tips, to which have been attached diamonds, decorations, favors, and gifts. There is a gift particular to everyone. Can you be so foolish as not to recognize and thank the one who offers such wonderful favors and gifts from behind the veil of the Unseen?

If you do not recognize him, you must argue: "The strings themselves make and offer these diamonds and other gifts." In that case, you must attribute to each string the status and function of a king [who has a miraculous power and knowledge to do whatever he wishes]. And all this, while before our very eyes an unseen hand is making the strings and attaching gifts to them!

Given the latter fact, everything in this palace points to that miracle-working one rather than to itself. If you do not recognize him, by denying what is occurring in the palace, you show a determined ignorance of a kind to which a truly human being must not sink.

NINTH PROOF: Come, O friend. You neither recognize nor want to recognize the palace's owner because you deem his existence improbable. You deny because you cannot grasp his wonderful art and manner of acting. But how can all of these exquisite things, this wonderful existence, be explained without recognizing him? If we recognize him, all this palace and its abundant contents are as easy to understand as a single thing in it.

If we do not recognize him and if he did not exist, one thing would be as hard to explain as the whole palace, for everything is as skillfully made as the palace. Things would not be so abundant and economical. No one could have any of these things that we see. Look at the jar of jam attached to that string.[17] If it had not been miraculously made in his hidden kitchen, we could not have bought it at any price. But now we buy it for a few cents.

Every kind of persistent difficulty and impossibility follows from not recognizing him. A tree is given life from one root, through one law, and in one center. Therefore, forming thousands of fruits is as easy as forming one fruit. If this depended on different, particular centers and

---

[17] The jar of jam denotes Mercy's gifts (melons, watermelons, pomegranates, and coconuts like tins of milk), each of which is a conserve of Divine Power.

roots and on separate, particular laws, each fruit would have been as hard to form as the tree. If an army's equipment is produced in one factory, through one law, and in one center, it is done as easily as equipping one soldier. But if each soldier's equipment is procured from many places, then equipping one soldier would require as many factories as needed for the whole army.

This is also true in this well-organized palace, splendid city, progressive state, and magnificent world. If the invention of all these things is attributed to one being, it is easy to account for their infinite abundance, availability, and munificence. Otherwise everything would be so costly and hard that the whole world would not be enough to buy a single thing.

TENTH PROOF: My friend, we have been here for 15 days.[18] If we still do not know and recognize this world's rules, we deserve punishment. We have no excuses, because for 15 days we have not been interfered with, as though given respite. But neither have we been left to ourselves. We cannot wander about and cause disorder among creatures so delicate, well-balanced, subtle, skill-

---

[18] An allusion to the age of 15, the age of responsibility.

fully made, and instructive as these. The majestic lord's punishment must be severe.

How majestic and powerful he must be to have arranged this huge world like a palace and turn it as though a light wheel. He administers this vast country like a house, missing nothing. Like filling a container and then emptying it, he continuously fills this palace, this city, this land with perfect orderliness and then empties it with perfect wisdom. Also, like setting up a table and then removing it, he lays out throughout the land, as though with an unseen hand, diverse tables with a great variety of foods one after the other, and then clears them away to bring new ones.[19] Seeing this and using your reason, you will understand that an infinite munificence is inherent in that awesome majesty.

Just as all these things testify to that unseen being's unity and sovereignty, so these revolutions and changes occurring one after the other

---

[19] The tables denote Earth's face in summer, during which hundreds of the Most Merciful One's tables are prepared fresh and different in the kitchens of mercy, and then are laid down and removed continuously. Every garden is a cooking pot, and every tree is a tray-bearer.

bear witness to his permanence. How so? For the causes of things disappear along with them, whereas the things we attribute to causes are repeated after them. So nothing can be attributed to causes; everything takes place as the work of an undying one. For example, sparkling bubbles on a river's surface come and go, but new ones coming after them also sparkle.

Therefore, what makes them sparkle is something constant standing high above the river and having permanent light. In the same way, the quick changes in this world and the things that replace the disappearing ones, assuming the same attributes, show that they are manifestations, inscriptions, mirrors, and works of art of a permanent and undying one.

ELEVENTH PROOF: Come, O friend. Now I will show you another decisive proof as powerful as the previous ten put together. Let's board the ship and sail to that peninsula over there, for the keys to this mysterious world are there.[20] Moreover,

---

[20] The ship refers to history, the peninsula to the place of Time of Happiness, and the age of the Prophet. Taking off the dress of modern civilization on the dark shore of this age, we sail on the ship of history over the sea of time, land on the Arabian peninsula in the Time of Happiness, and visit

everyone is looking to that peninsula, expecting something and receiving orders from there.

We have landed. Look at the huge meeting over there, as if all the country's important people have gathered. Look carefully, for this great community has a leader. Let's approach nearer to learn about him. See his brilliant decorations—more than a thousand.[21] How forcefully he speaks. How pleasant is his conversation. I have learned a little of what he says during these 15 days, and you could learn the same from me. He is speaking about the country's glorious miracle-displaying sovereign, who has sent him to us. See, he is displaying such wonders that we have to admit the truth of what he says.

Look carefully. Not only the peninsula's creatures are listening to him; he is making his voice

---

the Pride of Creation as he is carrying out his mission. We know that he is a proof of Divine Unity so brilliant that he illuminates the whole Earth and the two faces of time (past and future), and disperses the darkness of unbelief and misguidance.

[21] A thousand decorations signify the Prophet's miracles that, according to meticulous researchers, number around one thousand.

heard in wonderful fashion by the whole country. Near and far, everyone is trying to listen to his discourse, even animals. Even the mountains are listening to the commandments he has brought so that they are stirring in their places. Those trees move to the place to which he points. He brings forth water wherever he wishes. He makes his fingers like an abundant spring and lets others drink from them.

Look, that important lamp in the palace's dome splits into two at his gesture.[22] That means this whole land and its inhabitants recognize that he is an envoy. As though understanding that he is the most eminent and true translator of an unseen miracle-displaying one, the herald of his sovereignty, the discloser of his talisman, and a trustworthy envoy communicating his command-

---

[22] The important lamp is the moon, which split into two at his gesture. As Mawlana Jami remarked: "That unlettered one who never wrote, wrote with the pen of his finger an *alif* [the first letter of the Arabic alphabet] on the page of the skies, and made one forty into two fifties." In other words, before he split the moon, it resembled the Arabic letter *mim*, the mathematical value of which is forty. After splitting, it became two crescents resembling two *nuns*, the value of which is fifty.

ments, they heed and obey him. All around him, those who are sensible affirm whatever he says. By submitting to his commands and answering his beckoning, everything in this land, even the mountains, the trees, and the huge light that illuminates everywhere, affirm him.[23]

So, O friend, could there be any deception in the information brought by this most illustrious, magnificent, and serious of beings, who bears 1,000 decorations from the king's royal treasury? His words about the miracle-displaying king are said with total conviction and confirmed by all the country's notables, as is his description of the king's attributes and communication of his commands. If you think they contain some deception, you must deny the existence and reality of this

---

[23] The author refers to the mountains and trees answering the Prophet's call. See The Nineteenth Letter's ninth through twelfth signs in Said Nursi, *The Letters* (Turkey: The Light, Inc., 2002) (Tr.) The huge light is the sun. Once the Prophet was sleeping in 'Ali's arms, who did not wake him up out of deep love and respect for him. When the Prophet woke up, the sun was about to set, and 'Ali had not yet prayed the afternoon prayer. Upon the Prophet's order, Earth revolved a little backwards and the sun appeared above the horizon so 'Ali could pray. This is one of the Prophet's famous miracles.

palace, those lamps, and this congregation. Your objections will be refuted by the proof's power.

TWELFTH PROOF: You must have come to your senses a little. I will show you further proof as strong as the sum of the previous 11 proofs. Look at this illustrious decree,[24] which has descended from above and which everyone looks upon with full attention out of amazement or veneration. That being with 1,000 decorations is explaining its meaning.

The decree's brilliant style attracts everyone's admiration, and speaks of matters so important and serious that everyone feels compelled to listen. It describes all the acts, attributes, and commands of the one who governs this land, who made this palace, and exhibits these wonders. There is a mighty seal on the decree, an irresistible seal on every line and sentence. The meanings, truths, commandments, and instances of wisdom it provides are in a style unique to him, which also functions like a stamp or seal.

In short, this supreme decree shows that supreme being as clearly as the sun, so that one

---

[24] The illustrious decree refers to the Qur'an, and the seal refers to its miraculousness.

who is not blind can "see" him. If you have come to your senses, friend, this is enough for now. Do you have more objections?

The stubborn man replied: "In the face of all these proofs I can only say: 'All praise be to God,' for I have come to believe, in a way as bright as the sun and clear as daylight, that this land has a single Lord of Perfection, this world a single Owner of Majesty, and this palace a single Maker of Grace. May God be pleased with you for saving me from my former obstinacy and foolishness. Each proof is sufficient to demonstrate the truth. But with each successive proof, clearer and finer, more pleasant, agreeable, and radiant levels of knowledge, scenes of acquaintanceship, and windows of love were opened and revealed. I listened and learned."

The parable indicating the mighty truth of Divine Unity and belief in God is completed. Through the grace of the Most Merciful, the enlightenment of the Qur'an, and the light of belief, I will now show, after an introduction, 12 gleams from the sun of Divine Unity, corresponding to the 12 proofs in the parable. Success and guidance are from God alone.

Second station

Consider the following verses:

> In the name of God,
> the Merciful, the Compassionate.

> God is the Creator of everything, and He is Guardian over everything; unto Him belong the keys of the heavens and Earth. (39:62)

> So glory be to him, in Whose hand is the dominion of everything, and unto Whom you are being brought back. (36:83)

> There is not a thing but its treasuries are with Us, and We send it down but in a due and certain measure. (15:21)

> There is no creature that moves, but He takes it by the forelock. Surely my Lord is on a straight path. (11:56)

In my "Katra" (A Drop from the Ocean of Divine Unity's Proofs), which discusses belief in God, the first and most important of the pillars of belief, I briefly explained that every creature shows and bears witness to God's Existence and Unity in 55 ways.

In my "Nukta," I mentioned four universals out of the evidences for Almighty God's Existence and Unity. In my [12] Arabic treatises, I discussed hundreds of decisive proofs for All-Mighty God's Existence and Unity. Thus I will not discuss the matter here in great depth, but only relate 12 gleams from the sun of belief in God. I have written about these briefly elsewhere in the *Risale-i Nur*.

Twelve gleams

FIRST GLEAM: The affirmation of Divine Unity is of two sorts. For example, if an important, rich man's goods arrive in a market or a town, their ownership can be known in two ways. One is to look at them and conclude that only he could own so many items. If a regular person estimated or supervised them, much might be stolen or others might claim partial ownership. The second way is to read every packet's label and recognize every roll's stamp and every bill's seal. This allows one to conclude that everything belongs to that person, for everything points to him.

In exactly the same way, there are two kinds of affirmation of Divine Unity. One is the believer's superficial and common affirmation: "God Almighty is One, without partner or like. This universe is His." The other is the true affirmation. By seeing His Power's stamp, His Lordship's seal, and His pen's inscription on everything, one opens a window directly onto His light from everything.

The person then confirms and believes, with almost the certainty coming from direct observation, that everything comes into existence by His Power's hand, that He has no partner or helper in His Divinity and Lordship or His absolute Sovereignty. Through this, one attains a degree of permanent awareness of the Divine Presence. I will now mention some "rays" to prove that everything shows God's Unity.

NOTE: Divine Dignity and Greatness require material or natural causes to veil Divine Power's operations. The real agent acting in the universe is the Eternally-Besought-of-All's Power. Divine Unity and Majesty, as well as God's absolute independence and transcendence, require this. The Eternal Sovereign's officials, all that conveys His commands (e.g., air, angels, or natural causes), are not executives through whom He exercises His Sovereignty, but heralds of His Sovereignty and, as with angels, observers and superintendents of His acts as Lord—Sustainer, Administrator,

Upbringer, and Trainer—of the Worlds. They exist because they make known Power's dignity and Lordship's majesty, so that base and lowly things should not be attributed directly to Power.

Unlike a human king, who is essentially weak and destitute, God Almighty does not use officials to exercise His authority. Although everything seemingly occurs according to the principle of cause and effect, this is to preserve Power's dignity in the mind's superficial view.

Like a mirror, everything has two faces. One looks to the visible, material world, resembles the mirror's colored face, and may be a way to account for various "colors" and states. The other face is like the mirror's shinning face and looks to and consists of the inner dimension of things, where Divine Power operates directly.

In the apparent, material face of things, there may be states that are seemingly incompatible with the dignity and perfection of the Eternally-Besought-of-All's Power. In this face, Divine Power veils His operations behind cause and effect so that those states may be ascribed to causes. But in reality and with respect to the inner dimension of things, everything is beautiful and transparent.

It is fitting that Power should be associated with that dimension of things, which is not incompatible with Its dignity. Thus the function of causes is purely apparent, for they have no effect in respect to this dimension.

Another reason for apparent causes is that people tend to judge superficially. They raise unjust complaints and baseless objections about things or happenings that they find disagreeable. Almighty God, Who is totally just, has put causes in this material dimension of existence as a veil between such things or happenings and Himself so that such comments should not be aimed at Him. The faults and mistakes that make things and events disagreeable essentially originate in people themselves.

Here is a meaningful illustration of this subtle point: Azrail, the Angel of Death, once said to God Almighty: "Your servants will complain about and resent me, for I take their souls." God Almighty told him: "I shall put the veil of disasters and illnesses between you and my servants so that they will complain of them and not resent you." Thus illness is a veil to which people can attribute that which is disagreeable about death.

However disagreeable in appearance, death is in reality good and beautiful, and the essential beauty lying in it is attributable to Azrail's duty.

But Azrail is also an observer, a veil to Divine Power, so that people should attribute to him those aspects of death that their superficial reasoning cannot reconcile with Divine Mercy's perfection. Divine Dignity and Grandeur require that causes veil Divine Power's hand, while Divine Unity and Majesty demand that causes withdraw their hands from the true effect.

SECOND GLEAM: Look at this garden of the universe, this orchard of Earth. Notice the heavens' beautiful face, gilded with stars. Each creature scattered and spread out in them bears a stamp unique to the Maker, the Creator of all things. Each species bears illustrious and inimitable seals, all of which belong to the All-Majestic Maker, the All-Beautiful Creator, that are "written" on the pages of night and day, spring and summer, and published by Divine Power's Pen. I mention only a few as examples.

Consider the stamp He placed on life: He makes everything out of one thing and one thing out of many things. He makes the countless members and systems of an animal's body out of fertilizing sperm-bearing fluid and also out of simple drinking water. To make everything out of one thing is surely the work of an Absolutely All-Powerful One. Also, One Who transforms with perfect orderliness all substances contained in innumerable kinds of vegetable or animal food into particular bodies, weaving from them a unique skin for each and various bodily members, is surely an All-Powerful and Absolutely All-Knowing One.[25]

The Creator of life and death administers life in this workshop of the world according to His Wisdom. He uses such a miraculous law issuing from the sphere (realm) of His Creative Commands, that to execute and enforce it is a function unique to Him Who holds the universe in the grasp of His administrative Power and absolutely unconditioned authority. Thus, if you can reason

---

[25] Countless beings eat the same kinds of food and are composed of the same elements, and yet each one has a unique face, fingerprints, character, ambitions, feelings, and so on. This is irrefutable proof of the Existence and Unity of an All-Knowing and All-Powerful Creator Who has absolute Will and can do whatever He pleases in whatever way He wills. (Tr.)

and have a heart that "sees," you will understand that producing everything from one thing with perfect ease and order, and skillfully making many things into one thing with perfect harmony and orderliness, is a stamp unique to the Maker, the Creator of everything.

If you see that, together with weaving 100 rolls of broadcloth and other materials like silk and linen from one dram of cotton, a wonder-working one also makes many foods from it like helva and pastries; and if you see that he skillfully makes gold out of iron and stone, honey and butter, water and soil, which he holds in his hand, you will conclude that he has a special art, a particular way of working, and that all earthly elements and substances are subjugated to his command and authority. Truly, the manifestation of the Divine Power and Wisdom in living forms is far more wonderful and amazing than this example. This is only one out of many stamps on living forms.

THIRD GLEAM: Look at the living creatures moving in this ever-moving universe, in these revolving bodies. The Ever-Living and Self-Subsistent One has placed many seals on each one. One of them is this: A person is a miniature of the universe, a fruit of the Tree of Creation, and a seed of this world, for each person comprises samples of most species of beings. It is as if each living being were a drop distilled from the universe with the most subtle and sensitive balance. To create this living being and be its Lord requires that the creator have full control over the universe.

Can you not understand that to make a honeybee (a word of power) a sort of small index of most things, to "write" on humanity (a page) most of the universe's features, to include in a tiny fig seed (a point) an entire fig tree's program, to exhibit in our heart (a letter) the works of all Divine Names manifested throughout the universe, to record in human memory, which is situated in lentil-sized place, enough "writings" to fill a library, and to include in it a detailed index of all events in the cosmos, is most certainly a stamp unique to the Creator of all things and the All-Majestic Lord of the universe?

Thus if one seal of Lordship on living beings displays its light and makes His signs read in such a fashion, consider all those seals together. How can you not proclaim: "Glory be to Him Who is hidden by the intensity of His manifestation."

FOURTH GLEAM: Look carefully at the various multicolored beings floating in the heavens' "ocean" and scattered over Earth's face. Each one bears the Eternal Sun's inimitable signatures. Just as His seals on life and living beings are apparent, so are His signatures on His act of giving life. As comparisons make profound meanings more easily understood, I offer a suitable comparison.

Consider the sun: From planets to drops of water, to fragments of glass and sparkling snowflakes, a signature from the sun's image and reflection, a radiant work (effect) particular to the sun, is apparent. If you do not accept the tiny suns apparent in these innumerable things as manifestations of the sun's reflection, you must accept the absurd statement that an actual sun exists in each item.

In just the same way, and with respect to the giving of life from among the Eternal Sun's manifestations, He has placed such a signature on each living being. Even if all causes came together and each one was a free agent able to do whatever it wills, they could not imitate that signature.

Living beings (miracles of Divine Power) are each a focal point for the Divine Names' manifestations, which are like the Eternal Sun's rays. If, therefore, that amazing inscription of art, that curious composition of wisdom, that manifestation of the mystery of Oneness displayed by living beings is not attributed to the Single and Eternally Besought One, it means falling into total misguidance and superstition.

For example, it would mean giving each living creature an infinite creative power, an all-embracing knowledge, and an absolute will by which to govern the whole universe. In short, each one would have all the eternal attributes unique to the Necessarily Existent One. As such, each atom of that item would have to be divine, for each atom, especially seeds, are given such a character or properties that they take up a position in exact accordance. It is as if they are directly related with the whole species to which the living being growing from it belongs, for a seed seems to act in such a way that it is planted exactly in the place suitable for the continuation of its species and to plant the species' flag.

We may even say that the seed takes up a position so that the living being can continue its transactions and relations with all the other creatures with which it is connected to receive its necessary sustenance. If, then, that seed or atom does not act under an Absolutely Powerful One's command and its connection with Him is severed, it would have to have an eye with which to see all things and a consciousness encompassing all things.

In short, if the sun's images or reflections in water drops, glass fragments, and multicolored flowers are not attributed to the sun, we must accept the existence of innumerable suns. This is an inconceivable superstition. In the same way, if everything that exists is not attributed to the Absolutely All-Powerful One, we must accept the existence of as many gods as particles in the universe. Such an idea is clearly untenable.

In summary, then, each atom has three windows opening onto the Eternal Sun's light of Unity and Necessary Existence.

FIRST WINDOW: A soldier has relations with all levels of an army, duties in accordance with those relations, and actions in accordance with those duties and army regulations. It is the same with each atom in your body. For example, an atom in your eye's pupil has similar relations and duties with your eyes, head, powers of reproduction, attraction and repulsion; with your veins and arteries, motor and sensory nerves that circulate your blood and work your body; and with the rest of your body. This shows that each bodily atom is a work of an Eternal, All-Powerful One and operates under His command.

SECOND WINDOW: An air molecule may visit, enter, and work within any flower or fruit. If it were not subjugated to and working under an Absolutely All-Powerful One's command, it would have to know all systems and structures of all flowers and fruits and how they are formed, down to their peripheric lines. So that molecule shows the rays of a light of Divine Unity like a sun. The is true for light, soil, and water. Science says that the original sources of things are hydrogen, oxygen, carbon, and nitrogen. All of these are the components of soil, air, water, and light.

THIRD WINDOW: The seeds of all flowering and fruit-bearing plants are composed of carbon, nitrogen, hydrogen, and oxygen. The only difference is the program of their progenitor deposited in them by Divine Destiny. If we put different kinds of seeds in a pot filled with soil, which is composed of particular or certain elements, each plant will appear in its own wonderful form, shape, and amazing members.

If those particles were not subjugated to and under the command of One Who knows each thing with all its features, structures, lifecycles, and conditions of its life; One Who can endow everything with a suitable being and all that it needs; and to Whose Power everything is subjected without the least resistance, the following conclusions could not be avoided:

- Each soil atom would have to contain "immaterial factories" that determine all the plants' future lives as well as a number of workshops equal to all flowering and fruit-bearing plants, so that each could be the origin for these various beings. Do not forget that each plant differs in form, taste, color, and members.

- Each plant would have to have an all-encompassing knowledge and be able to form itself. In other words, if a being's connection with Almighty God is severed, you must accept a number of gods equal to the number of soil particles. This is untenable.

However, when you admit that the particles are working under an All-Powerful and All-Knowing

One's command, everything becomes very easy. An ordinary soldier, in the name of a powerful king and by relying and depending upon his power, can force a whole people to migrate, join two seas [by having them build a canal], or capture another king. In the same way, by the Eternal King's command and permission, a fly may kill a tyrant, an ant may destroy another tyrant's palace, and a fig seed may bear the load of a fig tree.[26]

Each atom contains two further true witnesses to the Maker's necessary Existence and Unity. Despite its absolute powerlessness, each atom performs many significant duties; despite its lifelessness, each atom displays a universal consciousness by acting in conformity with the universal order. Thus each atom testifies, through its impotence, to the Absolutely All-Powerful One's necessary Existence and to His Unity by acting in conformity with the order of the universe.

Each living being also contains two signs that He is the One and Eternally-Besought-of-All. In each is a seal of Divine Unity and a stamp of His being the Eternally-Besought-of-All, for each liv-

---

[26] A fly, entering Nimrod's nose and reaching his brain, caused him to die, and ants destroyed Pharaoh's palace.

ing being reflects in the mirror of itself all the Divine Names manifested in most parts of the universe. Like a focal point, it reflects the Ever-Living One's and the Self-Subsistent One's manifestations, two of the Greatest Divine Names. Since it reflects a display of the Unity of the Divine Essence behind the veil of the Name the Giver of Life, it bears a stamp of Divine Unity.

Again, since a living being is like a miniature of the universe and a fruit of the Tree of Creation, the easy satisfaction of its endless needs shows that God is the Eternally-Besought-of-All. In other words, the being has a Lord Who is concerned with it and always cares for it. Such concern and care is far more valuable for it than everything in the universe.

[God's care] suffices a thing against everything, while all things [even if banded together] cannot suffice even a single thing against Him. This shows that the Lord of all beings needs nothing, that satisfying their needs does not diminish His Wealth, and that nothing is difficult for His Power. This is a sort of stamp of His being the Eternally-Besought-of-All. Through the tongue of life, every living being recites: *Say: "He is*

God, the One. God, the Eternally-Besought-of-All" (112:1-2).

There are other significant windows or openings. I will discuss them briefly. Seeing that each atom opens up three windows and two openings on the Necessarily Existent One's Unity and that life opens two doors, understand how the levels of all beings radiate the light for knowing the All-Majestic One. From this you can understand the degrees of progress in knowledge of God and the degrees of peace attained through it.

FIFTH GLEAM: One pen is enough to write a book by hand. To print it, however, hundreds of metal "pens" must be arranged for each page. Further, if most of the book is to be inscribed in an extremely fine script within certain letters, as *Sura Ya Sin* can (and has been) written within the initial two letters of *Ya* and *Sin*, smaller "pens" are necessary. In the same way, if you accept that this Book of the Universe belongs to the One Who has written it with His Power's Pen, you follow a way so easy as to be necessary and inevitable. But if you attribute it to causality or nature, you follow a way so hard as to be impossible, and so riddled with superstition that even a most fanciful mind could not accept it.

Claiming that nature is self-created means that each soil atom, water drop, and air molecule contains millions of printing machines and infinite "immaterial factories" [to substitute for Destiny in determining the lives of all things in nature], so that nature could originate all flowering and fruit-bearing plants [and govern their lives]. Or else there should be an all-encompassing knowledge and a power able to do everything in each air, water, and soil atom so that nature really could create itself.

Most plants can grow in any soil if there is enough water and air. But their formation and structure is so systematic, balanced and well-ordered, and their forms are so unique, that a specific factory or "printing machine" would be necessary for each one. To create itself, therefore, nature would need a specific "machine" to create each item. It is very hard to find people who accept such a superstition.

In short, every letter of a book points to itself only to the extent of being a letter and to only one aspect of its existence and meaning. However, it describes its writer and shows him in many ways—for example: "The one who wrote me has fine penmanship. His pen is red." In the same way, each letter of this vast Book of the Universe points to itself to the extent of its size and form, but describes the Eternal Designer's Names as elaborately as an ode, testifies to Him, and points to His Names with its "index fingers" (its qualities). Thus nobody, not even foolish Sophists who deny themselves and the universe, can deny the All-Majestic Maker.

SIXTH GLEAM: Just as the All-Majestic Creator has placed the stamp of His Unity on His creatures' foreheads, He has placed in a most visible fashion many stamps of His Unity on all species, numerous seals of His Unity on all kingdoms of beings, and various signatures of His Oneness on the whole world. Out of these let's look at one placed on Earth's face in spring. This stamp of Divine Unity is as evident and brilliant as spring, during which the Eternal Designer resurrects countless plant and animal species with complete differentiation and specification, and perfect orderliness and separation amid infinite intermingling and confusion.

Is it so hard to perceive that raising dead soil to life in spring, showing with perfect order countless samples of resurrection, and writing on Earth's page the individual members of countless species without fault or forgetting, mistake or deficiency, and in a most well-balanced and well-proportioned, well-ordered and perfect fashion, is a seal unique to One of Majesty, an All-Powerful One of Perfection, an All-Wise One of Grace and Beauty, One Who has infinite Power, all-encompassing Knowledge, and a Will able to govern the universe?

> Look upon the signs and imprints of God's Mercy, how He revives Earth after its death. He will revive the dead [in the same way]. He is powerful over all things. (30:50)

Resurrecting the dead is such a simple matter for the Creative Power that, within a few days, gives countless examples of this by quickening Earth. For example, is it proper to ask a miracle-working one who, at a sign, raises up Mount Ararat if he can remove a huge rock blocking your way? In the same way, is it proper to say (in a manner implying doubt) to an All-Wise and Powerful One, an All-Munificent and Compassionate One, Who created the firmaments, Earth and the mountains in "6 days" and continuously fills and empties them: "Can you remove this layer of soil over us that is blocking our way to Your banquet prepared and laid out in eternity? Can you level it and let us pass across it?"

Surely you have seen a stamp of Divine Unity on Earth's face during summer. A seal of Divine Oneness is clearly seen in the most wise, insightful, and mighty Divine operations on Earth's face during spring. This activity is absolutely extensive, speedy, liberal or generous, and done in absolute orderliness. A most perfect beauty of art, it is done in a most perfect form of creation. Thus only One with infinite knowledge and boundless power could own such a seal. That seal belongs to One Who, although nowhere, is all-present and all-seeing. Nothing is hidden from or difficult for Him. With respect to His Power, particles and stars are equal.

Once in a garden of the All-Compassionate One of Grace's munificence, I counted bunches (of grapes) hanging from a grapevine that was two-fingers thick. I saw it to be like one little pip among the "bunches" of His miracles. There were 155 bunches, and one bunch contained about 120 grapes. I thought: If this grape vine were a tap from which honeyed water flowed ceaselessly, only then would the water be enough, in this heat, for the bunches on which hang those hundreds of little "pumps" of mercy's sherbet. But this grapevine manages with only a little moisture, which it occasionally obtains. Therefore the One Who does this must be powerful over all things. Glory be to Him at whose work minds are bewildered.

SEVENTH GLEAM: With a little care and effort, you can see the Eternally-Besought-of-All's seals on Earth's "page." When you raise your head to look at the great Book of the Universe, you will see on it a seal of Divine Unity as big and clear as itself. Like a factory's components or a palace's building blocks, all creatures support, aid, and work together—in perfect orderliness—to meet each other's needs. Joining efforts, they serve living beings. Cooperating, they obey an All-Wise Administrator toward one goal. Obeying the rule of mutual assistance, which is in force throughout the universe, they demonstrate to thoughtful people that they act through the power of a single, Most Munificent Upbringer and at the command of a single, Most Wise Administrator.

Such mutual support and assistance, answering of each other's needs, close cooperation, obedience, submission, and order testify that all creatures are administered through a single Administrator's organization and directed by a single Upbringer. Also, the universal providence and favor included in the universal wisdom, which is clearly apparent in the purposeful creation of things, as well as the comprehensive mercy evident from the providence and the universal sustenance required by that mercy to feed all living beings, form a seal of Divine Unity so brilliant that anyone with sight and thought will see and understand it.

A fabric of wisdom showing intention, consciousness, and will covers the universe; a fine net curtain of providence and favor showing grace, adornment, embellishment, and kindness is placed above it; over that is spread a robe of mercy radiating the will of being known and loved, of favoring with bounties and gifts enveloping the universe; and over that is laid a table of provision for maintaining all creatures, which shows Lordship's kindness, bestowal, benevolence, perfect caring, proper nurturing, grace, and favoring. All of this clearly shows an All-Gracious One Who is All-

Wise, All-Generous, All-Compassionate, and All-Providing.

Is everything in need of sustenance? Yes, they are. Like an individual being needing food to live, all beings, especially living beings, whether universal or particular or wholes or parts, have many material and immaterial demands and needs that must be met if they are to continue living. Although they cannot obtain even the smallest need, we see that all their needs are met, in an unexpected way and from an unexpected source, with perfect order, at the appropriate time, in a suitable fashion, and with perfect wisdom. Does this not clearly show an All-Wise Nurturer of Majesty, an All-Compassionate Provider of Grace?

EIGHTH GLEAM: Seeds sown in a field show that the field and the seeds belong to the one who owns both. Likewise, life's fundamental elements (e.g., air, water, and soil) are universal and omnipresent despite their simplicity and sameness. Plants and animals, which are fruits of Mercy, miracles of Power, and words of Wisdom, also are found everywhere despite their essentially similar nature vis-à-vis life's diverse conditions. This shows that they belong to a single miracle-displaying Maker and that every flower, fruit, and animal is a stamp, a seal, and a signature of that Maker.

Regardless of location, each one says in the tongue of its being: "The One Whose stamp I bear also made this location. The One Whose seal I carry also created this place as a missive. The One Whose signature I indicate also wove this land." Only the One Who holds all elements in His Power's grasp can own and sustain the least of creatures. Those who are not blind can see that only One Who exercises Lordship over all plants and animals can own, sustain, and govern the simplest one of them.

In the tongue of similarity to other individuals, each individual being says: "Only the one who owns my species can own me." In the tongue of spreading over Earth's face with other species, each species says: "Only the one who owns Earth's face can be our owner." In the tongue of being bound to the sun, with other planets, and of its mutual relations with the heavens, Earth says: "Only the one who owns all these can be my owner."

Suppose apples were conscious and that someone said to one of them: "You are my work of art." The apple would exclaim: "Be quiet! If you can form all apples on Earth; rather, if you have power over all fruit-bearing trees on Earth and over all the gifts of the All-Merciful One proceeding from the treasury of Mercy, only then can you claim Lordship over me!"

NINTH GLEAM: After indicating some of the seals, stamps, and signatures on particulars and parts, universals and wholes, as well as on the world, life, living beings, and on the giving of life, I will indicate one of the infinite stamps on species.

Since a tree's countless fruits depend on one law of growth from one center, they are as easy and cheap to raise as a single fruit. In other words, multiple centers would require for a single fruit as much hardship, expenditure, and equipment as for a whole tree, and manufacturing the needed military equipment for one soldier would require all factories for a whole army. The first case explains the extraordinary ease of creating all species from a center of unity; the second case shows the impossible and countless difficulties that arise if creation were dependent upon multiple centers.

In short, therefore, the correspondence and similarity in basic members between a species' members and a genus' divisions proves that they are works of a single Maker, as they are "inscribed" with the same Pen and bear the same seal. The absolute ease of their creation, which makes them necessary and inevitable, requires that they be the work of One Maker. Otherwise, the ensuing difficulties would doom that genus and that species to non-existence.

Given this, attributing everything to Almighty God makes all things are as easy as one thing; when attributed to causes, one thing is impossibly difficult. Thus the extraordinary economy and ease seen in the universe, as well as the endless abundance, clearly show the stamp of Unity. If these abundant and cheap fruits did not belong to the One of Unity, we could not buy a pomegranate even if we gave the world in exchange. How could we pay for the purposeful and conscious cooperation of the various universal elements (e.g., soil, air, water, sunlight, heat) and the seed, all of which are unconscious and obey a Single Maker, Who is Almighty God? The cost of a pomegranate or any other fruit is the whole universe.

TENTH GLEAM: Just as life, which shows Divine Grace, is an argument and proof for Divine Unity, even a sort of display of Divine Unity, death, which shows Divine Majesty, is an argument and proof for Divine Oneness.[27]

Consider this: Bubbles on a mighty river reflect the sun's image and light, as do transparent objects glistening on Earth's face. Both testify to the sun's existence. Although the bubbles sometimes disappear (such as by passing under a bridge), successive troops of bubbles continue to show the sun's reflection and display its light. This proves that the little images of the sun, which appear, disappear, and then reappear, point to an enduring, perpetual, single sun that continues to manifest itself from on high. Thus, those sparkling bubbles demonstrate the sun's exis-

---

[27] Oneness (*Ahadiya*) and Unity (*Wahidiya*) differ. Oneness means the concurrent manifestations of all or most of the Divine Names on one thing. For example, life is the result of the manifestations of many Names, such as the Creator, Fashioner, All-Favoring, All-Merciful, and All-Providing. Unity means the manifestation of a Divine Name on all things, as death is common to all living beings and results from the manifestation of the Divine Name the One-Who-Causes-To-Die. (Tr.)

tence and display its continuation and unity through their disappearance and extinction.

In the same way, the existence and life of these beings in continuous flux testify to the Necessarily Existent Being's necessary Existence and Oneness, as well as to His Unity, eternity, and permanence, via their decay and death. The beautiful, delicate creatures that are renewed and recruited along, with the alternation of day and night, summer and winter, and the passage of centuries and ages, show the Existence, Unity, and permanence of an elevated, everlasting One with a continuous display of beauty.

In the same way, their decay and death, together with the apparent causes for their lives, show that (material or natural) causes are only veils. This proves that these arts, inscriptions, and manifestations are the constantly renewed arts, changing inscriptions, and moving mirrors of an All-Beautiful One of Majesty, all of Whose Names are sacred and beautiful. Also, they are His stamps that follow one after the other, and His seals that are charged with wisdom.

This Book of the Universe instructs us in the signs of Divine Existence and Unity seen in the universe's creation and operation, and bears witness to all the All-Majestic One's Attributes of Perfection, Beauty, Grace, and Majesty. These signs also prove the essential Perfection of Divine Being, without fault and defect, for a work's perfection points to the perfection of the act lying in that work's origin. The act's perfection points to the name's perfection, which points to the attribute's perfection, which points to the essential capacity's perfection, which necessarily, intuitively, and evidently points to the perfection of the one with that essential capacity.

For example, a perfect palace's perfect design and adornments show the perfection of a masterbuilder's acts. The acts' perfection show the perfection of the eminent builder's titles, which specify his rank. The titles' perfection show the perfection of the builder's attributes, which are the origin of the art. The perfection of the art and attributes show the perfection of the master's abilities and essential capacity. The perfection of those essential abilities and capacity show the perfection of the master's essential nature.

In the same way, the faultless works seen in the universe, about which the Qur'an asks: *Do you see any flaw?* (67:3), the art in the universe's well-ordered beings, point to an Effective, Powerful Agent's perfect acts. The acts' perfection point to the perfection of that Majestic Agent's Names. The Names' perfection points and testifies to the perfection of the Attributes of the Majestic One known with the Names. The Attributes' perfection points and testifies to the perfection of the essential capacity and qualities of the Perfect One qualified by those attributes.

The perfection of the essential capacity and qualities point to the perfection of the One having such capacity and qualities with such certainty that all types of perfections observed throughout the universe are but signs of His Perfection, hints of His Majesty, and allusions to His Beauty in the forms of pale, weak shadows when compared to His Perfect Reality.

ELEVENTH GLEAM AS RADIANT AS THE SUN: As shown in The Nineteenth Word, our master Muhammad[28] the Trustworthy is the supreme

---

[28] In any publication dealing with Prophet Muhammad, his name or title is followed by "upon him be peace and blessings," to show our respect for him and because it is a religious requirement. For his Companions and other illustrious

"verse" of the great Book of the Universe, the "Greatest Name" of God shown in that "Qur'an" of the cosmos, the seed and most illustrious fruit of the Tree of Creation, the sun of the palace of the world, the luminous full moon of the world of Islam, and the herald of Divine Lordship's sovereignty. He is the wise discoverer of creation's secret, the one who flies through the levels of truth on the wings of Messengership, which embraces all previous Prophets, and of Islam, which takes under its protection the world of Islam.

With the support of all Prophets and Messengers, saints and truthful, truth-seeking scholars and purified ones, he attested to Divine Unity with all his strength and opened the way to the Divine Throne. What fancy or doubt can divert belief in God, which he demonstrated, and close this way to Divine Unity, which he proved?

Since I described, to some extent, that clear proof and miracle-working being through 14 droplets from the water of life of his knowledge in

---

Muslims: "May God be pleased with him (or her)" is used. However, as this might be distracting to non-Muslim readers, these phrases do not appear in this book, on the understanding that they are assumed and that no disrespect is intended. (Ed.)

The Nineteenth Word, and through 19 signs in The Nineteenth Letter (on his miracles), I conclude with calling God's blessing on him as testimony to his truthfulness.

> O God, bestow blessings on the one who leads to the necessity of Your Existence and Your Unity, and testifies to Your Majesty and Grace and Perfection; the truthful and confirmed witness, and the verified, articulate proof; the lord of Prophets and Messengers, the bearer of the meaning of their consensus, affirmation, and miracles; the leader of saints and fruitful ones, who has the meaning of their agreement, verifications, and wonder-working; and the one with evident miracles, clear wonders, and decisive proofs that corroborate and affirm him.
>
> [O God, bestow blessings on] the one with exalted virtues in his person, elevated morals in his duty, and lofty qualities in his Shari'a, perfect and free of all contradiction; the center where Divine Revelation descended, as agreed upon by the One Who revealed, what was revealed, and the one who brought the Revelation to him; the traveler through the worlds of the Unseen and the inner dimensions of things; the observer of spirits, who conversed with angels; and

the sample of all the perfections in creation, in regard to individuals, species, and genera (the Tree of Creation's most illustrious fruit).

[O God, bestow blessings on] the lamp of truth, the proof of reality, the embodiment of mercy, the model of love, the discoverer of the secret of creation, the herald of the sovereignty of Divine Lordship, the one who demonstrated through the sublimity of his spiritual personality that he was before the "eyes" of the Author of the World at the creation of the universe, and the one who brought a Shari'a that shows through the comprehensiveness and soundness of its principles that it is the order of the Composer of the world and established by the Creator of the universe.

The One Who composed the universe with this perfect order composed this religion [Islam] with its finest and most beautiful order. He is our master, master of the communities of the children of Adam; our guide to belief, the communities of believers, Muhammad ibn 'Abd Allah ibn 'Abd al-Muttalib, upon him be the best of blessings and the most perfect peace as long as Earth and the heavens subsist. As the leader of all other

> witnesses and instructor of all human generations, this truthful and confirmed witness witnessed and announced with all his strength, utmost solemnity, utter steadfastness, strength of certainty, and perfection of belief: "I bear witness that there is no god but God, the One. He has no partner."

TWELFTH GLEAM AS RADIANT AS THE SUN: This twelfth gleam is such an ocean of truths that all 22 Words are only 22 drops in it; such a source of light that they are only 22 rays in it. Each Word is only a ray from one of the stars of the verses shining in the heavens of the Qur'an. Each is a drop from the river of a verse flowing from that Ocean of the Distinguisher between Truth and Falsehood, a pearl from a verse, each of which is a chest of jewels in the greatest of treasuries: God's Book.

This word of God is defined a little in the The Nineteenth Word's 14 droplets. Originating in His Greatest Name, it descended from the Supreme Divine Throne as the greatest manifestation of Divine Lordship. So elevated and comprehensive as to encompass and then even transcend time and bind the ground to the Supreme Divine Throne, it repeatedly declares with all its strength and its verses' absolute certainty: "There is no god but

God." Making the universe testify to this, all of its contents sing in unison: "There is no god but God."

If you look at the Qur'an with the eyes of a sound heart, you will see that its six sides are so brilliant and transparent that no darkness and misguidance, doubt, suspicion, or deception can penetrate it. Nor is there a fissure through which such things could infiltrate into the sphere of its purity. Above it is the stamp of miraculousness, beneath it proof and evidence, behind it its point of support—pure Divine Revelation, before it happiness in this world and the next, on its right questioning human reason about its truth and ensuring its confirmation, and on its left calling the human conscience to testify to its truth and securing its submission. In its inside is the pure guidance of the All-Merciful One, and on its outside is the light of belief.

Its fruits, with the certainty depending on observation, are the purified and truth-loving scholars and saints, adorned with all human perfections and attainments. If you listen to that Tongue of the Unseen—the Qur'an—you will hear from its depths a most familiar and convincing, an infinitely solemn and elevated, heavenly voice furnished with proofs repeatedly declaring: "There is no god but He." It states this with such absolute certainty depending on actual experience and complete conviction, that, about its truth, it gives you certainty of knowledge to the degree of certainty coming from direct witnessing and observation.

In short, the Messenger and the Most Firm Criterion to distinguish between truth and falsehood (the Qur'an) are each a "sun." The former, the tongue of the visible, material world, along with the support of 1,000 miracles and confirmation of all Prophets and purified scholars, points with the fingers of Islam and Messengership to the truth of "There is no god but God" and shows it with all his strength. The latter, the tongue of the Unseen world, having 40 aspects of miraculousness and confirmed by creation's Divine signs and the universe's operation, points to the same truth with the fingers of right and guidance, and shows it in a most solemn manner. Thus that truth is clearer than the sun and more manifest than daylight.

O obstinate one immersed in misguidance, who attempts to deny and annul the Qur'an! How can you oppose these suns with your mind's dim lamp? How can you remain indifferent? Are you trying to extinguish them by blowing? Enough of your denying mind! How can you deny the words and claims spoken by the Qur'an and the Prophet in the Name of the Lord of all the worlds and Owner of the universe? Who are you that you attempt to deny the Majestic Owner of the universe?

Conclusion

O friend with an alert mind and an attentive heart. If you have understood this Word, take these 12 gleams in your hand so that you might obtain a lamp of truth as light-giving as thousands of electric lights. Hold fast to the Qur'anic verses descending from God's Supreme Throne. Climbing on the "mount" of Divine assistance, ascend to the heavens of truth. Rise to the "throne of Divine knowledge" and declare: "I bear witness that there is no god but You. You are One, without partner."

Also declare:

> There is no god but God, One, having no partner; His is the dominion of all existence, and to Him belongs all praise; He alone gives life and causes to die; He is living and dies not; in His hand is all good; and He is powerful over everything. Glory be to You. We have no

knowledge save what You have taught us. Truly You are the All-Knowing, the All-Wise. Our Lord, do not call us to account if we forget or fall into error.

Our Lord, do not lay on us a burden like that which You laid on those before us. Our Lord, do not impose on us that which we cannot bear. Pardon us, forgive us, and have mercy on us. You are our Protector. Give us victory over the people of disbelief. Our Lord, do not cause our hearts to swerve after You have guided us. Bestow upon us mercy from Your Presence, for You are the Bestower. Our Lord, You are He who will gather humanity together on a Day of which there is no doubt. God never fails in His promise.

O God, bestow blessings and peace on the one whom You sent as a mercy for all the worlds, and on his Family[29] and Companions. Have mercy on us and his community, for the sake of Your Mercy, O most Merciful of the Merciful. Amen.

The conclusion of their call will be: "All praise be to God, the Lord of the Worlds."

---

[29] The Prophet's Family: The Prophet, Ali, Fatima, Hasan, and Husayn. These people are known as the *Ahl al-Bayt*, the Family (or People) of the House. The Prophet's wives are not included in this designation. (Tr.)

THE THIRTY-SECOND WORD

Divine Unity and Oneness • Human Happiness and Misery

(NOTE: This Word consists of three Stations. The First Station is an appendix explaining the Eighth Gleam of The Twenty-second Word and interpreting the first of the 55 languages by which universal entities bear witness to God's Oneness. It also discusses one truth, in the form of an imaginary conversation, of the many truths expressed in: *Had there been gods in either [Earth or the heavens] besides God, both would surely be in disorder* [21:22].)

Three stations

In the name of God,
the Merciful, the Compassionate.

First station

Had there been gods in either [Earth or the heavens] besides God, both surely would be in disorder.

> There is no god but God, He alone; having no partner; His is the Kingdom and to Him belongs all praise; He alone gives life and makes to die; He is living and dies not; in His hand is all good. He is powerful over everything, and unto Him is the homecoming.

One night during Ramadan I mentioned that each of those eleven statements of affirmation of Unity contained an aspect of Divine Unity and a particular good tiding (for believers). I explained only the meaning of *without partner* in the form of an allegorical conversation. Now, at the request of brothers at the mosque and friends attending me, I have committed this conversation to writing.

Imagine someone who, on behalf of unbelievers (who attribute everything to nature or material causes, or are polytheists or atheists), presumes to be Lord or exercise Lordship by alleging that he or she owns or rules, controls or disposes of a part of creation. Coming upon an atom, he or she informs it in the language or according to the presumptions of materialistic science or natural philosophy that he or she is its true master and owner. The atom answers in the language of truth and revealed wisdom:

I perform many tasks, and work within, alongside, or upon an infinite variety of created, ever-evolving entities. Do you have the knowledge and power to direct me in these tasks? I work and move in a measured relationship with innumerable other atoms of a like constitution.[30] Can you command and employ all of these? If you own, arrange, or manage the infinite complexity of entities of, for example, red blood corpuscles, of whose atoms I am but one, and do so with perfect knowledge and discipline, then presume to be my master, and only then presume me to be attributable to any other than God.

But you cannot do so, so be silent! You do not own me and cannot interfere in my

---

[30] Each mobile object, from tiny particles to planets, shows the Eternally-Besought-of-All's stamp and Unity. Also, by virtue of its motion, each takes possession of the places in which it enters in Unity's name, thus adding them to the property of its true Owner. Each immobile entity, from plants to fixed stars, is like a seal of Unity that shows its location as missives of their Maker. Each plant and fruit is a stamp and seal of Unity that argues, in Unity's name, that its habitat and native place is the missive of its Maker. In short, by moving in Unity's name, each entity takes possession of all entities, which means that one who cannot master all stars cannot master a single particle.

> operation, for all of my movements and activities are so purposeful and arranged that only One with infinite Wisdom and all-encompassing Knowledge can run them. If any other had a hand in it, there would be confusion. How can anyone who, like you, cannot even give yourself life, whose seeing and feeling are blind to truth, who sees yourself as subject to chance and accidents of nature, even presume to interfere in my functioning?

The pretender responds as all materialists do: "Be your own master then! Why do you claim to be in the service of some other power?" The atom replies:

> If I had a mind with knowledge as all-encompassing as the sun's light and with power as intense as its heat; if I had powers of feeling as all-embracing as the seven colors in its light; if I had faces and eyes to turn to every being and every place with which my being and my place are connected; and if I had authority in and over all these connections—then perhaps, perhaps, I might have claimed to be my own master.
>
> Yet even then, had I done so, I only would have been as foolish as yourself. Now get away from me, for you have no business with me!

The pretender, giving up on the atom, looks for a particular and harmonious grouping of atoms in the cell of a living body. Coming upon a red blood corpuscle (and thinking he or she can grasp its nature and control its workings), he or she speaks to it in the name of material causality and the language of natural philosophy: "I possess you. I am your master, and you work for me." The red blood corpuscle answers in the language of truth and Divine Wisdom:

> But I am not alone. If you also possess all my fellows in the blood army with whom I share the same formation pointing to our Maker, as well as the same duties and functions, and if you have the full and detailed knowledge, the awesome and subtle power, as well as the perfect wisdom to direct all the body cells through which we move and in which we operate, there might be some sense to your pretensions.
>
> But as you depend on blind and deaf nature or natural forces, you can have no influence over us, let alone mastery over me. Our order is as perfect as it is intricate. Only One Who sees, hears, and knows all things forward and backward in time and in all directions of space; only He Who governs the being and

> operation of all that is; only He could be our true sovereign and master. So go your way, for I have better and more important things to do than answer your nonsensical pretensions!

Unable to deceive the red blood corpuscle, the pretender moves on and comes across a larger entity they call "cell." Addressing it in the familiar language of natural philosophy, he or she says: "True, the atom and the red blood corpuscle did not listen to me. I hope you can understand me. As I can see, you are composed of several smaller elements, like things arranged in a room. I can have a hand in this arrangement, and arrange and rearrange it. You can be my creature, and I can have power over you." The body cell answers with wisdom and in the language of truth:

> Although I am small, I perform vital tasks. I have the subtlest and yet strongest connections with all my neighboring cells, and with the whole organism of which I am a part. I perform vital functions with, for example, arteries and veins, sensory and motor nerves, electrical forces of attraction and repulsion, and the principles or elements determining my size, shape, and reproduction.

If you have the knowledge and power to form an entire organism, to order and regulate the arteries and veins and nerves, and to put to work all the diverse forces and principles managing our form and function; if you can direct, with irresistible power and all-comprehending wisdom, the innumerable body cells similar to me in artistry and quality, then show your ability. Then perhaps, perhaps, you might claim to master or make me.

But as you cannot, leave me—there are even now red blood cells carrying nourishment for me, white blood cells confronting diseases that might threaten me—I am busy, so do not waste my time any further with your vanity. No one as empty as you are of true understanding, of true hearing and seeing, could ever meddle in our being. Our order is so precise, delicate, and perfect that only One with absolute Wisdom, Knowledge, and Power could control us.[31] If it were oth-

---

[31] The All-Wise Maker has created the human body like a well-ordered city. Nerves function as telephones and telegraphs, while some of the blood vessels function as pipes carrying water to a fountain through which blood (the water of life) flows. Blood contains two types of corpuscles: red ones convey nutrients to the body's cells, their suste-

erwise, our cohesion and order would not exist or would quickly fall into chaos.

Disappointed, the pretender seeks out a still larger entity and, confronting a human body, reiterates the argument in the language of unenlightened nature and erring philosophy: "I can say that you are mine, that I have a share in owning and managing you." The human body answers in the language of wisdom and truth and in the "natural" tongue of its order:

> Do you have the knowledge and power to control and direct all human bodies similar to me that manifest the same signs of supreme power and creation? Do you have dominion over the treasuries of light, air, and water, as well as of all plants and animals, which are the ground and store of my provision and sustenance?
>
> Do you have the boundless wisdom and infinite power by which such invaluable, immaterial entities as the mind, intellect,

---

nance, according to a Divine law (analogous to merchants and officers distributing food); white ones, fewer in number, defend (analogous to soldiers) against such invaders as disease. When actively engaged in defense, they perform two revolutions like Mawlawi dervishes and display a striking and rapid fluidity.

> and soul are so securely disposed in a narrow, bodily envelope, such as me, and made to "worship" by performing extremely important tasks? If you have such power, knowledge, and wisdom, demonstrate it—only then claim to own and manage me.
>
> But as you cannot, be silent! My Maker is All-Powerful, All-Knowing, All-Seeing, and All-Hearing—this is testified to by the perfection with which I am organized and by the sign of Oneness in my face. A being as ignorant and incompetent as you could never have the least hand in His art.

The pretender, nonplussed that all points in the human body reject his or her claim to have a say, moves on and surveys humanity as a species, thinking:

> They live in such diverse and complex societies—I see that the devil finds a way to interfere in their affairs of will and their social relations. Is there a way for me to enter into the creation, constitution, and operation of their bodies? If I can find such a point, I will be able to control the body and its cells that turned me down.

With this intention, he or she addresses the species in the familiar language of blind nature and erring philosophy: "You appear very diverse and at great odds. I am your master and owner or, at the very least, have a share in your making." Humanity responds in the language of truth and reality, and in the tongue of wisdom and order:

> Do you have the power, knowledge, and wisdom to create the rich texture covering Earth's face, woven with perfect wisdom from varied fabrics, thousands of mineral and plant and animal species, including humanity? Can you, with a like wisdom, renew this texture and do so continuously? Do you possess the all-extensive power and all-comprehending science that manages Earth, of which we are a fruit, and the universe, of which we are the seed?
>
> Can you send us, from across the universe and in measured amounts, the provisions we need for our sustenance? Can you generate all individuals of my kind, past and future, whose faces bear the same sign of supreme majesty as mine? If so, you might then, perhaps, claim mastery over me.
>
> But as you cannot, be silent! Do not dare to say that you have a hand in me just from remarking the diversity in my kind, for that diversity is part of our ordering's

perfection. Diversity and multiplicity are copies made with a perfect order from the Book of Destiny [containing the origins of beings in a perfect order] by Power. Our diversity of appearance is a sort of reproducing of our forms [dictated by Destiny]—as the perfect diversity and order of plants and animals (which are inferior to us, under our vigilance, and which we study) also testifies.

Is it at all plausible that the One Who weaves the diverse fabrics spread over and through this world's texture with great skill is other than its Maker, that the Creator of a fruit is other than the Creator of the tree from which it grows, and that the Creator of a seed is other than the Creator of the fruit it yields?

You are blind, for you do not see the miracles of His Omnipotence in my face and the wonders of His Creation in my constitution. If you had seen, you would have understood that nothing escapes my Maker's observation or tasks Him capriciously. He makes the stars as easily as He makes an atom. He creates springtime as smoothly as He creates a flower. He has placed the vast universe's index in my constitution with perfect correspondence. Could anyone who is, as you are, corporeal, incompetent, blind, and deaf have had a hand in such a Being's artistry? So be silent, and be gone!

The pretender then turns to the widespread texture overlaying Earth's face like an embellished cloak and speaks to it in the name of causality and in the language of natural philosophy: "I can manage you. I own you, or at least have a share in you." The texture answers in the name of truth and in the language of wisdom[32]:

> If you have the skill and power to create and weave all textures that have been hung on the line of past time, laid, unlaid, and relaid seamlessly throughout all time, and that will be hung on the line of future time, according to programs and patterns predesigned with the greatest precision and in accordance with Destiny's framework, each elegant, purposeful, and uniquely adorned; if you possess immaterial hands that can reach out from Earth's creation to its destruction, or rather, from the eternity of no-

---

[32] In fact, the texture is animated, continuously giving the signs of life in a regular fashion. Its embroideries are renewed continuously with perfect wisdom and order to display the various, ever-differing manifestations of its Weaver's Names.

> beginning to the eternity that is to come; if you have the power and science to create all individuals within this texture, restoring and renewing them in exact order and wisdom; if you can create and possess Earth itself which is, as it were, a model for me and puts me on like a veil—only if you can, only then claim mastery over me—if not, leave! You have no business here!
>
> In my rich and harmonious diversity are demonstrated clear signs of Oneness, and the clear stamp of His Uniqueness. Only He Who controls the whole cosmos, Who can do innumerable tasks simultaneously, Who can see all beings and their actions, whether inner or outer, at the same instant, Who is present and vigilant everywhere while being unbounded by time, space, or dimension, and who has infinite wisdom, science, and power—only such a Being could ever own or have dominion over me.

The pretender turns to Earth, hoping to deceive it,[33] and repeats the same argument in the

---

[33] Briefly, beginning with the particle or atom, each thing visited referred the pretender to the next level: from the particle or atom to the red blood corpuscle, the cell, the body, humanity, Earth's outer garment, Earth as a globe, the sun,

name of causality and in the language of mere naturalism: "I see that you roam about idly in the universe. Certainly you can have no master, and so I claim you." Upon hearing this, Earth roars like thunder in the name of truth:

> Do not be foolish! How can I roam about without a master? Have you ever seen any disorder, lack of wisdom or skill, in the making of my dress or in any little point or fabric of it, that you dare to say that I roam about idly? Do you presume to own my orbit, which would take some 25,000 years to traverse at a human being's pace but which I complete in my annual round with perfect discipline and precision?[34]
>
> Do you claim to own my ten fellow planets, which carry on their appointed

---

and the stars, respectively. Each said: "Be off! If you can subjugate the next one up from me, do so, and then return and seek to master me. If you cannot subjugate that level, you also cannot subjugate me!" Thus one whose authority does not embrace stars has no acceptable claim to mastery over a single particle.

[34] If half the diameter of a circle is roughly 180 million kilometers, the circle covers a distance of roughly 25,000 years [to cover on foot, provided one covers 4 kilometers (2.4 miles) an hour and walks for 5 hours a day.]

> tasks along their individual orbits as I do? Do you claim to have the unlimited science and power to create and control the sun, which gathers and focuses our orbits, orbits to which we are bound through the gravitation of mercy, and to make me and other planets revolve around it?
>
> Since you cannot plausibly make such a claim, leave me, for I have work to do. Our awesome circling, purposeful submission, and magnificent discipline show that our Maker is a Being to Whom all entities submit, and submit perfectly—as a dutiful soldier submits to his superior's orders. He is the Wise and Absolute Ruler of Majesty, Who holds the sun and planets in their proper order as easily as He adorns each tree with its proper fruit.

Having failed to find a place in governing Earth, the pretender turns to the sun in the expectation that he or she can open a path there. Since the sun is so great an entity, he or she hopes to use it to gain control of Earth. Addressing the sun in the name of the way of associating partners with God Almighty and in the language of satanic philosophy, as sun-worshippers do, the pretender says: "You are a monarch. You are your own master. You do whatever you will." The sun answers in the name of truth and reality and in the language of Divine Wisdom:

> No, indeed! How can you utter such an untruth! I am but an obedient officer, no more than a candle in my Master's guest-house. I could not own so much as a fly, even its wing, for even such a small thing has such immaterial faculties and fine, exquisite works of art as its eye and ear. I do not have their like in any of my workshops. I cannot make even the smallest of them.

Though rebuked by the sun, the pretender argues in the manner of Pharaohs, arrogant creatures who promote themselves as deities: "I claim you as mine in the name of causality, since you are not your own master but merely a servant." The sun replies in the name of truth and in the language of obedience to its Creator: "I can belong only to that Being Who has created me and all resplendent stars like me, Who, having fixed them in their stations with perfect wisdom, rotates them in glory and adorns the wide heavens thereby."

The pretender then comes among the stars and thinks: "Perhaps I can find some clients here." Talking to them in the name of causality and its partners and in the language of corrupt philosophy as star-worshippers do, he says: "You must be under the control of many different rulers, seeing that you are situated at such vast distances from each other." Upon this, one star, speaking for all others, answers him:

> How senseless and mindless you must be, not to see or understand the signs of the Creator's Oneness and the stamp of His Uniqueness in our nature. Do you not know how absolute is our organization, how secure the laws we obey? You think we have no order. In fact, we are the handiwork and servants of a Unique and Indivisible Being Who holds the sky (our sea), the cosmos (our tree), and the vastness of space (our wide, maneuvering field) in His control. Like the many-colored lamps indicating human festivities, we are luminous witnesses of His perfect Dominion, brilliant evidence blazing across boundless space, of His Kingdom and Lordship.
>
> Each of us is a shining servant displaying His Majesty, near and far, in this world and the next, and in the many worlds beyond, within the infinitude of His Creation. Each of us is a miracle from the Power of the One, a perfectly ordered

fruit on the Tree of Creation, a bright manifestation of God's Unity, a home and mount and mosque for His angels, a lamp and a sun of higher worlds, an ornament, a flower, a palace of the celestial sphere, a luminescent fish in the heavenly ocean, and each a beautiful eye set in the face of the heavens.[35] Throughout our vast community there exists profound silence amidst tranquillity, movement in wisdom, light ornament with majestic grandeur, the most varied beauty in perfect harmony, and the highest art in absolute balance.

Since you accuse us of disorder and empty distances, of having no duty and no master, while we proclaim in innumerable tongues the Unity of our Majestic Maker and His being the Eternally-Besought-of-All, together with His Attributes of perfection, grace, and beauty—since you accuse us, whose purity is unstained, whose obedience and servanthood are perfect, you merit a slap

---

[35] In other words, we are only pointers beholding the wonders of the Almighty's creation and pointing others to behold them. The heavens observe the wonders of Earth's Divine artistry with innumerable eyes. As angels do in the skies, stars observe Earth, a display hall of wonders, and their doing so urges conscious beings to observe it attentively.

in the face in payment for your absurd effrontery!

The star strikes the pretender's face in a gesture like the stoning of the devil, and hurls him from the stars' domain to the bottom of Hell. It also hurls natural philosophy into the storms of uncertainty,[36] and chance into the well of non-existence. It hurls all who arrogate to themselves some portion in the One God's Dominion into the utter darkness of improbability and impossibility, and every argument against true religion into the lowest of the low.

Then the stars together recite the holy decree: *Had there been gods in either (Earth or the heavens) besides God, both would be in disorder* (21:22), and affirm: "There is no place for any partner with God, neither in the interstices of a

---

[36] After its lapse, nature repented. Understanding that its proper purpose and obligation is not to be active and cause effects, but rather to receive and to be acted upon, it realized that it is a sort of notebook of Divine Determining, susceptible to mutation and change; a sort of program of the Lord's Power, analogous to the corpus of rules of creation instituted by the All-Powerful of Majesty, an assemblage of His laws. It assumed its duty of worship in perfect submission, admitting its absolute powerlessness and therein achieved the title of God's creation and the Lord's handiwork.

fly's wing nor amid the heavens' stars and spaces."

> Glory be to You! We have no knowledge save what You have taught us. You are All-Knowing, All-Wise.
>
> O God, bestow peace and blessings on our master Muhammad, the lamp of Your Unity amidst the multiplicity of Your creatures, and the herald of Your Oneness in the display hall of Your universe, and on his Family and Companions.

***

In the Name of God,
the Merciful, the Compassionate.

Look at the imprints of God's Mercy, how He revives Earth after its death! (30:50)

The following points to a flower from the eternal garden of this verse:

> Every tree in blossom is an ode
> rhythmic and well-composed,
> singing the high and manifest praises of the Creator.
> Or something with multiple eyes opened to watch,
> and cause others to watch the wonders
> of the Maker's art displayed.
> Or has clothed its members in green
> for their festival so that its Lord may observe
> His illustrious works and gifts upon it,
> while itself displays in the display hall—
> Earth—His Mercy's embellishments before

> humanity's eyes, thereby proclaiming the
> wisdom in its creation, in that significant
> treasuries are stored in it by the Grace and
> Generosity of the Sustainer of its fruits:
> Glory be to Him, how generous His favoring,
> how clear the arguments for Him,
> how manifest are His proofs!

The imagination sees angels clothed in bodies from the (branches of) these trees resembling thousands of flutes, from which are heard songs of praises of the All-Living One. Each leaf is a tongue reciting: "O Living One," and chanting all together: "There is no god but He."

> Say: "O God, Master of the Kingdom, You give kingdom to whomever You will and withdraw kingdom from whomever You will."

They incessantly utter: "O Truth," announce: "O All-Living One," and together proclaim: "God."

> We send down from heaven blessed water. (50:9)

A SHORT ADDENDUM

Listen to the following verse:

> Do they not look at the heaven above them, how We have built it and adorned it? (50:6)

Look at the sky's face, where you see a silence in restful serenity, a purposive motion, radiance in majesty, a smile in adornment, all combined in creation's orderliness and art's symmetry. Its candle's brilliance, its lamp's dazzle, and its stars' glitter manifest infinite Sovereignty for those with insight and sound reasoning.

The following expounds the lines above in interpreting the verse (50:6): The verse draws attention to the sky's adorned and beautiful face. People who observe it with care must notice the silence in the extraordinary calmness and apparent rest observed there, and conclude that the sky has assumed that form through an Absolutely Powerful One's order and subjugation.

If the heavenly bodies roamed at random, with their enormous size and speed of motion, the resulting noise would deafen everybody. They also would cause such tumult and confusion that the universe would collapse. If 20 buffaloes move together in the same area, you can guess what great uproar and confusion they would cause. However, according to astronomers, some moving stars are 1,000 times larger than Earth and move at a speed 70 times faster than a cannonball.

Given this, from the silence of the heavenly bodies in calmness and rest, you may understand the extent of the Power of subjugation belonging to the Majestic Maker and the All-Powerful One of Perfection, and the degree of the stars' submission and obedience to Him.

A PURPOSIVE MOTION: The verse orders us to see the purposive motion in the sky. That extremely strange and mighty motion takes place in absolute dependence on an extraordinarily subtle and comprehensive purpose. The immensity and order of a factory whose wheels and machinery turn and toil in wisdom, in perfect order and for wise purposes, show to what extent its engineer is learned and skillful. In the same way, with the sun in the center and mighty planets revolving around it in a perfect, subtle order for many wise purposes, the solar system shows the extent of the All-Powerful One's Power and Wisdom.

RADIANCE IN MAJESTY AND A SMILE IN ADORNMENT: The sky contains a radiance of such majesty and a smile of such adornment that it shows the splendid sovereignty and beautiful art that the Majestic Maker controls. In the same way as innumerable illuminations used on special occasions to show the king's majesty and his country's advanced civilization, the vast heavens with their majestic glittering stars show to attentive eyes the perfection of the Majestic Maker's sovereignty and His art's beauty.

ALL COMBINED IN THE ORDERLINESS OF CREATION AND THE SYMMETRY OF ART: The verse says:

> See the order and balance in the sky and know how powerful and wise the Creator is. When you see someone turning numerous objects one round the other in a perfect order and with a special, delicate balance for many wise purposes, you may guess how wise, powerful, and skillful that one is. Likewise, together with their numberless stars of awesome size and speed, the vast heavens in their tremendous immensity have performed their duties for billions of years according to an established measure and with a certain, sensitive balance. They have never transgressed their limits, and have never caused even the slightest disorder. This shows to attentive eyes just how sensitive and exact is the measure according to which their Majestic Maker exercises His Lordship.

Like similar verses in *Surat al-Naba'*, among others, the verse also indicates that the Majestic

Divine Unity and Oneness • Human Happiness and Misery

Creator has subjugated the sun, moon, and other heavenly bodies.

ITS CANDLE'S BRILLIANCE, ITS LAMP'S DAZZLE, AND ITS STARS' GLITTER MANIFEST THE INFINITE SOVEREIGNTY FOR THOSE WITH INSIGHT AND SOUND REASONING: Almighty God has hung on the world's adorned roof a sun-like lamp that gives heat and light. He uses this as a "pot" of light to write the Eternally-Besought-of-All's "letters" on the lines of day and night on the pages of the seasons.

Like the luminous hour-hands of a clock in a tall tower, He has made the moon in heaven's dome the hour-hand of the largest clock of time. He causes it to move through its mansions according to a perfect measure and fine calculations, as if He leaves a different crescent to each night and then folds all of them in itself (making it invisible). Furthermore, He has gilded the sky's beautiful face with stars that glitter and smile in that dome. All this points to His Lordship's infinite Sovereignty and His Divinity's magnificence and invites thinking people to believe in His Existence and Unity.

> Look at the colorful page of the Book of the
> Universe, and see how the golden pen of the Power
> has inscribed it!
> No point has been left dark for those
> who can see with the eyes of their hearts.

It is as if God wrote His signs with light.
See what an astounding miracle of
wisdom the universe is!
See how tremendous a spectacle
the space of the universe is!
Listen to the stars and heed their beautiful sermons!
See what is written in these luminous
missives of Wisdom!
All of them are jointly delivering
this fruitful discourse:
Each of us is a radiant proof for the majestic
Sovereignty of an All-Powerful One of glory.
We bear witness to the Maker's Existence
and to His Unity and Power.
We are His subtle miracles sending light
to gild the face of the Earth, and on which the
angels make excursions.
We are the heavens' innumerable discerning eyes
directed to Paradise and overseeing Earth.
We are the exquisite fruits attached to
the heavenly branch of the Tree of Creation,
and to the twigs of the Milky Way, attached by
the Majestic, All-Gracious Being's hand of wisdom.
For the heavens' inhabitants we are traveling
mosques, revolving houses, and exalted homes,
light-diffusing lamps, mighty ships, planes.
We are miracles of the Power of the All-Powerful
One of Perfection, the All-Wise One of Majesty.
Each of us is a wonder of His creative art,
a rarity of His Wisdom, a marvel of His creation,
a world of light. To the one who is truly human,
we present countless proofs in countless tongues.
The atheists' eyes, may they be blind, never see our
faces, nor do their ears hear our speech.
We are signs that speak the truth.
On us is the same stamp and seal.
We obey and glorify our Lord,

> and mention Him in worship.
> We are ecstatic lovers in the Milky Way's widest
> circle, the circle reciting our Lord's Names.

Second station

> In the Name of God,
> the Merciful, the Compassionate.
>
> Say: He is God, the One,
> the Eternally-Besought-of-All.

This Station consists of three aims.

FIRST AIM: (Having been cast down by a star, the representative of those attributing partners to God gave up the attempt to find a part of creation that would accept him or her as God's partner. However, to incite doubt about God's Unity, he or she sought to arouse suspicions in the minds of its adherents by asking three questions.)

QUESTION: In the language of atheists, he or she asks: "I've found no evidence to prove my cause. But how can you prove the existence of a single One of infinite power? Why do you reject everything but His Power in the universe's creation and operation?

ANSWER: As was argued convincingly in The Twenty-second Word, each creature is a clear proof for the Necessarily Existent Being, the Absolutely Powerful One's necessary existence. Each link in the chain of creation proves His Unity. Among the many Qur'anic arguments, particularly like: *If you ask them who has created the heavens and Earth, they will certainly say: God* (39:38) and *Among His signs is the creation of the heavens and Earth, and the difference of your languages and colors* (30:22), the creation of the heavens and Earth is presented as a proof of God's Existence and Unity. Conscious people who consider the creation of the heavens and Earth must confirm the Majestic Creator's existence. When asked who their creator is, they will answer: "God."

In the First Station, we started from an atom and showed Divine Unity's stamp on every object as far as the heavens and the stars. The Qur'an rejects partnership with God. This means that (since the universe is like a person, for both are organisms whose parts work together and are interrelated), the Absolutely Powerful One, Who created the heavens and Earth in perfect order, must hold the amazing solar system in His Power's grasp.

Since that absolutely All-Powerful One holds the sun and its planets in His Power's grasp, managing it and regulating its movements, Earth must be in His Power's grasp and management. Given this, all of its creatures, which are its fruits and may be regarded as the goal of its existence, are in His Lordship's grasp (raising, administering, and sustaining).

All creatures, spread over Earth singly or in groups and replaced after adorning it for a while, fill and empty Earth in a continuous cycle. As all of them are in the grasp of His Power and Knowledge and are managed and arranged according to the measure of His Justice and Wisdom, each member of each species, each of which is a well-designed and perfectly formed miniature of the universe, a pattern or specimen of its species, and a tiny index of the Book of the Universe, are in His grasp of Lordship, invention, raising, and management.

Given this, each living being's cells, corpuscles, limbs, and nerves are under His command, at His disposal, and move according to His laws. Lastly, particles or atoms, the essential building blocks constituting all creatures and their parts as well as being the means for their design and formation, are in His Power's grasp and His

Knowledge's sphere. They move most regularly and perform perfect duties by His command, permission, and strength.

Every atom moves and functions by His law, permission, and command. Therefore, His Knowledge and Wisdom distinguish each face by making it unique. Also, their sounds and tongues differ. Consider this verse that, in mentioning only the first and most universal link and the last and most individualized one, points to this chain of creation and the series of His signs in creation:

> Among His signs is the creation of the heavens and Earth, and the difference of your languages and colors. Indeed, in this are signs for those who know. (30:22)

Now we say: "O representative of those associating partners with God! These evidences are as strong as the chains of creation, which point to an Absolutely Powerful One and prove His Unity."

Since the creation of the heavens and Earth shows an All-Powerful Maker and His boundless and infinitely perfect Power, He is absolutely independent of partners. While He has no need for them, why do you follow the dark way of associating partners with Him? As He has no partners in His Divinity, any partnership in His Lordship and creativity is impossible. The Power of the Maker of the universe and Earth is boundless and infinitely perfect, and everything is equal before it. If there were a partner, this would require that a limited power defeat a boundless and infinitely perfect power, or somehow limit it and infect it with incapacity. Such assertions are untenable.

There is no need for partners, and their supposed existence is inconceivable. Such claims are no more than forced and arbitrary judgments that cannot be substantiated by reason or logic. It is a principle of theology and methodology that any probability or possibility not arising from evidence cannot be considered, and that it does not injure conviction or certainty based on knowledge. For example, it is theoretically conceivable that Lake Egridir might change into oil or grape juice boiled to a heavy syrup. But since this is a mere possibility raised on the basis of no circumstantial evidence, it does not harm our certainty that the lake is water.

Similarly, we have asked each part of the universe: from atoms to stars in the First Station, and from the creation of the heavens and Earth to unique faces in the Second Station. Each part testified to God's Oneness and showed the stamp of His Unity. Therefore there is no circumstantial sign upon which any partnership with God could be found. Given that this claim is forced, meaningless, and insubstantial, all such claims are clear nonsense and pure ignorance.

QUESTION: Those who reject Divine Unity raise another issue: Everything depends on a cause and takes place according to the cycle of cause and effect. Since causality is apparent throughout the universe, causes must have a part in the creation and operation of things. If they have a part, they may be partners.

ANSWER: As required by Divine Will and Wisdom, and as the Divine Names tend to manifest themselves, results are dependent on causes. However, as is convincingly argued in the *Risale-i Nur,* causes have no creative effect. Here we add the following:

Conscious beings are the most effective causes in bringing about effects. Humanity, which has a free and most comprehensive willpower and a vast field in which to exercise it, is the most elevated conscious being. Speaking, thinking, and eating are the most apparent acts arising from our free will. They include well-ordered chains of events, but only one is directly connected to our free will. For example, out of all the processes related to eating and its becoming nourishment in cells, only chewing them depends on free will. Hunger, thirst, and appetite are external to free will, as is the body's independent working. In the case of speaking, free will is limited to inhaling and exhaling the air needed by the vocal organs to produce sounds. A word is like a seed in the mouth, becomes like a tree when uttered, produces millions of fruits that resemble that single word, and enters millions of ears. We can only imagine this multiplication, free will has nothing more to do with after it has been said.

If humanity, the most honored cause and agent, the freest in using will, has no part in creation, how can nature (e.g., inanimate objects, elements, plants, animals) have any real effect or part in creation? How can natural laws, which have no consciousness, will, or knowledge and only a nominal existence, originate such a miraculous system as the universe, the creation and operation of which require infinite knowledge, will, and power? How can they create a miraculous living, conscious, speaking, reasoning, thinking, and learning organism like a man or a woman?

Nature is only an envelope for the Lord's creatures, a tray for the All-Merciful One's gifts. The tray bearing the gift, the cloth in which it is wrapped, even the one who brings it, cannot be a partner in the king's sovereignty. One who does not understand this is blinded by delusion. In the same way, apparent causes and means have no part in Divine Lordship; their only duty is to worship.

SECOND AIM: (In despair, this being tries to demolish belief in Divine Unity through doubt.)

QUESTION: You argue that the universe's Creator is absolutely One and the Eternally-Besought-of-All. He is Single yet has absolute and free control of everything. He exercises His absolute authority over all things simultaneously and can do innumerable things at the same time. How can we believe such a bewildering assertion? How can one being do countless things in countless places at the same instant and without difficulty?

ANSWER: Our answer requires that we analyze an extremely profound and subtle, as well as very elevated and comprehensive, mystery of God's being One and the Eternally-Besought-of-All. The mind can discern that mystery only by comparison. Although His Essence and Attributes have no like or equal and are not comparable, His acts may be considered through comparison.

First comparison: As argued convincingly in The Sixteenth Word, people can acquire universality through various mirrors. While being particular in essence, they can be universal by having numerous aspects at the same time. Just as things like glass and water become universal in those mirrors, more refined and transparent matters (e.g., air, ether, certain objects from the World of Symbols and Immaterial Forms) become like mirrors to bodies of light and spirit beings. Such matter carries them, allowing them to travel as fast as lightning and imagination.

Seated on them, these bodies of light and spirit beings travel with the speed of imagination in such clear realms as the World of Immaterial Forms and can be present in thousands of places at once. Since they are of light and their reflections are identical with themselves and have exactly the same qualities, they act in every place as if they were personally present. The reflections of solid, corporeal bodies are not identical with themselves and, not having the same qualities as themselves, are lifeless.

For example, the sun is a concrete particular object that acquires universality by shining on transparent objects. It lends its reflections and images to all shining things on Earth according to each one's capacity. Even a drop of water and a piece of glass reflect the sun's image. The sun is present, through its light, heat, image, or the seven colors in its light, everywhere on Earth.

If it had knowledge and consciousness, each object, especially shining and transparent ones, would be like a seat or chair through which it could contact everything. It also would be able to communicate with all conscious beings, through mirrors or each one's eye, while communicating with all others. While present and acting everywhere on Earth through its knowledge, power, and other attributes, it would be nowhere in person.

The sun is only like a solid, particular, and lifeless mirror to the Name the Light out of the Majestic Being's 1,001 Names. It is honored with such universal functions. Thus despite His Being Single in Essence, why should the Majestic Being be unable to do countless things at the same time?

Second comparison: Since the universe is like a tree, each tree may be an example of the universe's realities. Taking the huge tree in front of my room as a tiny specimen of the universe, we shall demonstrate Divine Singleness' manifestation in the universe. This tree has at least 1,000 fruits, and each fruit has at least 100 seeds. All fruits and seeds were created at the same time. However, that tree has the same single node of its nucleus of life in its original seed, roots, and trunk. This node contains the laws of its formation issuing from Divine Will and Divine Command, and permeates all parts of the tree by being present in each fruit and seed.

Unlike light, heat, and air, this nucleus of life, which is a single display of Divine Will and a law of Divine Command, does not dissipate but it is present in every part. Its manifold actions are not contrary to its singleness. In fact, the manifestation of Divine Will, that law of Divine Command and nucleus of life, may be present in each part and nowhere at the same time. It is as if that law of Divine Command had as many eyes and ears as that magnificent tree's fruits and seeds. Or it is as if each part of the tree had a control center for the "senses and feelings" of that law of Divine Command. The tree's veins and parts, such as branches, are like telephone wires in facilitating that law's operation or functioning.

Given that a single particular manifestation of God's Attribute of Will is observably the means of millions of acts in millions of places at the same time, we are convinced, as if seeing it with our own eyes, that the Majestic Being controls the Tree of Creation and all of its parts and atoms by manifesting His Power and Will.

As convincingly argued in The Sixteenth Word, such single, fixed, and helpless luminaries as the sun, restricted by matter, and His laws of Command and manifestations of His Will, such as those comprising the nucleus of that tree's life, move according to God's laws and are seen to be in many places and performing numerous tasks simultaneously. Although each such object is a particular thing restricted by matter, it resembles a universal thing and can accomplish many things at once. You see this with your own eyes, and so cannot deny it.

The Sacred Being is free of matter, exempt

from restrictions and the darkness of density. All lights and luminaries, as well as all creatures of pure light, are a single shadow of His Sacred Names' lights. Existence and life; the worlds of spirits, immaterial forms, and symbols; and the Intermediary World of the grave are semi-transparent mirrors of His Beauty and Grace. His Attributes are all-encompassing; His acts are universal.

How can something hide from Him, Who is Single, Who manifests His Attributes and acts through His universal Will, absolute Power, and all-encompassing Knowledge? What can be hard for or concealed from Him? Who can be far from Him or draw near to Him without acquiring universality? What can prevent Him from doing something else?

As Ibn 'Abbas pointed out, why should He not have immaterial eyes and ears that can look at and hear creatures? Why should chains of things not be like veins or wires that quickly convey His laws and commands? Why should things considered obstacles and impediments not be the means of His free disposition of creation? Why should causes and means not be only apparent veils (to His direct control of the universe and free operation)?

Why should He not be present everywhere and not contained by any place? Why should He need to reside in a certain place? Why should distance, size, or veils of the levels of existence be obstacles to His nearness to things, or to seeing and controlling them as He wishes?

Why should change, alteration, containment by space, and division (all intrinsic qualities of physical, restricted, contingent, solid, and multiplying beings) be accidental or necessary to the Sacred Being, the Light of Lights, the Single One of Unity, the Necessarily Existent One, Who is free of matter and restriction, exempt from defect and fault? Does impotence ever befit Him? Does defect ever appear in His Honor and Dignity?

Conclusion of the Second Aim: Reflecting on God's Singleness while looking at the fruit tree in front of my room, the following series of reflections occurred to me:

Glory be to Him Who has made the garden of His Earth a display hall of His art. He uses it to exhibit His Wisdom, manifest His Power, cause

His Mercy to blossom, the seeds of His Paradise to be sown, and His creatures to come and depart.

Adorned animals, ornamented birds, fruit-bearing trees, and flowering plants are miracles of His Knowledge, wonders of His art, gifts of His Munificence, and offerings of His Favoring. Flowers smiling because of beautiful fruits, birds singing at the dawn breeze, raindrops glittering on flowers' cheeks, mothers' compassion for their infants—all of this because the All-Loving One wills to make Himself known, the All-Merciful One wills to make Himself loved, the All-Compassionate One wills to make His Compassion known, and the All-Favoring One wills to make His Affection recognized by humanity, jinn, angels, and other spirit beings.

Each fruit and seed is a miracle of Divine Wisdom, a wonder of Divine art, a gift of Divine Mercy, a proof of Divine Oneness, and a sign of God's bounties in the Hereafter. They are true witnesses of His all-comprehensive Power and all-inclusive Knowledge, as well as mirrors to His Oneness in this World of Multiplicity, for in the tongue of its being, each one says: "This elaborate tree is included in me. Don't be absorbed in its elaboration. All its parts and features are encapsulated in me." A seed is like the fruit's heart, a mirror to Divine Oneness. In the tongue of its being, it "recites" in its heart the Divine Names recited by the entire tree.

Seeds are also signs of Divine Destiny and embodied symbols of Divine Power. Through them, Destiny indicates and Power alludes to the fact that each elaborate tree has grown from one seed and so points to its Maker's Oneness, Who has no partner in its creation and fashioning. After it has grown and elaborated itself fully, it encapsulates all its laws, realities, and life-history in a fruit. As all of its meaning is contained in a seed, it shows the Majestic Creator's wisdom in His creation and government.

As in the case of that tree, Oneness also is the source of the Tree of Creation's existence and growth. Similarly, being the fruit of the universe, humanity points to Unity in the multiplicity of beings, and the human heart sees the meaning of Unity in multiplicity with the eye of belief.

These fruits and seeds are also tablets of

Divine Wisdom through which Wisdom speaks to conscious beings like this:

> This tree's life and the efforts spent for its growth are aimed at its fruits, which represent it and is the aim of its growth. Its life is aimed at the seeds, because each seed is an index bearing the tree's entire meaning.
>
> Thus, the One Who creates the tree and the necessary conditions for its growth aims all manifestations of His Names concerned with the tree's life at the fruit, the *raison d'être* of its existence. Furthermore, that huge tree is sometimes pruned to control its growth and make it yield better fruits for many years; they cut off some parts of it so that it may rejuvenate.

Similarly, as we are the Tree of Creation's fruit, we are the reason for the universe's creation and existence, and the human heart is the most illumined and comprehensive mirror of the Maker of the universe. Due to this, humanity undergoes frequent pruning in the form of convulsions, revolutions, upheavals, and physical and social change, and it will cause the destruction and reconstruction of the universe. The door of this world will be closed and the door of a new one be opened for its judgement.

Here it is appropriate to explain a point showing the eloquence and force of Qur'anic expressions dealing with the Resurrection. As argued above, the universe must be destroyed and a new one built to judge humanity. There is a Power that will do this. However, the Resurrection will be done in stages. We must believe in and acquire knowledge of some of those stages. In order to perceive and acquire knowledge of other stages, we must evolve spiritually and intellectually. To prove the simplest stage, the Qur'an draws our attention to a Power that will open up the Resurrection's broadest sphere.

This is the simplest stage that all people must know and believe in: When people die, their spirits go to other abodes. Their bodies rot underground, but a tiny part (a seed) remains intact. During the Resurrection, God recreates us from it and returns the spirit to it.

This stage is so easy that countless examples of it are seen every spring. Many Qur'anic verses call our attention to the operations of a Power that will gather and then disperse all atoms. Sometimes they show the works of a Power and Wisdom that will send creation into non-existence and then recreate it, or rend the heavens asunder and scatter the stars. They also show the operations and manifestations of a Power and Wisdom that will make to die and then revive all living creatures at once through a single call, or the works of a Power and Wisdom that will toss mountains into the air, completely level and then reshape the world in a new and more beautiful form.

This means that, together with the phase in which all people will be recreated and which all people must believe in and have knowledge of, Almighty God will perform all tasks connected with the Resurrection with the same Power and Wisdom.

QUESTION: You often use analogies in the form of parables in *The Words*. According to logic, such analogies do not offer certainty, and issues requiring conviction for belief must be based on logical proofs. Analogy is used in jurisprudence for potential solutions and for cases in which a fairly certain presumption is enough. Furthermore, you set forth analogies and comparisons as parables, which by definition are not real.

ANSWER: According to logic, analogies do not

offer certainty. But one type of analogy is stronger than logical proof and gives greater certainty than deduction: Using a particular analogy to point to the tip of a universal truth and basing your conclusion on that truth. To teach that truth and deal with particular incidents and realities in accordance with it, you show the general or universal law on which the truth is based in a certain, particular object.

For example, through the analogy that the sun is a single body that can be present in all shining objects at once because it emits light, we show the law of a truth: Light and things of light are not restricted. Distance, size, and quantity make no difference to such items, and they cannot be contained in space.

A tree's leaves and fruits are formed easily and perfectly at the same time and in the same center through a law of Divine Command. This shows the tip of a mighty truth and a universal law, and proves that truth and law. Like a tree, this vast universe is the result of that law and the manifestation of oneness. All analogies and comparisons in The Words are of this kind. They offer greater conviction and certainty than logical proofs.

As for the second part, according to the science of eloquence, a metaphor is a word or phrase used to suggest or express a meaning other than its original one. In such statements, the metaphorical (and not the original) meaning is considered. If the metaphorical meaning conforms to reality, you are saying the truth. For example, height can be conveyed by the phrase: "The sheath of so-and-so's sword is long." If that man is tall, this statement is true whether or not he has such a sword. If he is not tall, this statement is false even if he has such a sword, for the phrase is only figurative in meaning.

Such parables as those in the Tenth and Twenty-second Words contain realities that are to be sought in metaphors. Their original meanings are like telescopes through which to see the truth being discussed. We speak in parables so that readers may understand subtle realities via such comparisons. However, to make them understandable to everyone, states and dispositions are presented in the forms of speeches, and the community's character is presented as a particular individual.

THIRD AIM: (Receiving a convincing answer

to the second question, the misguided one asks:)

QUESTION: Qur'anic expressions like the Best of Creators and the Most Merciful of the Merciful suggest the existence of others. Also, you assert that the Creator of the universe has infinite perfections by encompassing the highest degree of all perfections. But perfections are judged by way of contrast. Pleasure's perfection cannot be perceived without pain, light cannot be recognized without darkness, and union gives no pleasure if there is no separation.

ANSWER: We answer the first part via five indications.

First indication: Being a book that stresses Divine Unity, the Qur'an could not have used those phrases as you understand them. Rather, the Best of Creators means that the Creator has the highest rank of creativity. This does not suggest the existence of other creators for, like other Attributes, creativity has ranks of manifestation. Thus this phrase means that He is a Majestic Creator having the ultimate rank of creativity.

Second indication: Such phrases as *the Best of Creators* do not suggest a plurality of creators. Rather, they relate to species of beings and mean that He is a Creator Who creates everything in the best and most appropriate fashion. Verses like *He creates everything in the best form* (32:7) have the same meaning.

Third indication: Such phrases as *the Best of Creators, God is the Greatest, the Best of Judges,* and *the Best of the Benevolent* do not compare those acts and Attributes of God that are manifested in the universe with those of creatures, who manifest only their shadowy reflections. What-ever beings have is a gift from God. [We see because God is All-Seeing, and hear because He is All-Hearing.] All perfections shared by humanity, angels, and jinn are only indistinct shadows in relation to His, which are beyond compare.

People, especially the misguided, cannot measure God properly and are usually forgetful of Him. For example, a private respects his corporal but is oblivious of the king when he thanks the corporal for anything. He should be warned: "The king is greater than your corporal, so you must thank the king." Actually, everything ultimately comes from the king; the corporal is only an envoy. The king's actual, magnificent command cannot be compared with the corporal's. The only purpose for the warning, which contains a comparison, is to warn the private who prefers the corporal in gratitude and forgets the king.

Similarly, means, nature, and causes blind heedless people to the True Bestower of Bounties. They attribute the bounties which they receive to means and nature and creativity to causes, as if they were the actual sources, and praise and thank them. This is a sure path to associating others with God, and so the Qur'an warns: Almighty God is much greater and a far better Creator and Benefactor (actually meaning that He is the sole Creator and Benefactor). Regard Him and thank Him.

Fourth indication: Comparisons may be made between actually existent, possible, and even imagined things. People may imagine infinite grades in the Divine Names' and Attributes' essence. Almighty God is, however, of the highest, most perfect, and most beautiful of all grades that His Names and Attributes are imagined to have. The universe bears witness to this. His description of all His Names as the best or most beautiful, as in: *His are the Most Beautiful Names*

(20:8), points to this fact.

Fifth indication: Such phrases also should be considered from the following viewpoint. Almighty God has two kinds of Attributes and ways of manifestations. In the first one (*Wahidiya*), the form of an all-encompassing law, He shows His Names throughout the universe from behind apparent means and causes. In the second one (*Ahadiya*), He focuses His manifestations on one being without any means or veils. When shown in this second way, His kindness, creation, and grandeur are brighter, more beautiful and splendid than their manifestations in the first way.

Suppose a saintly king executes his authority directly. He can do so in two ways: by some general laws he has established and using officials and governors in every office, or via direct governance by being present everywhere at the same time in different forms and without officials. This second way is better and more excellent.

Similarly, the Creator of the universe, the Eternal King, uses means and causes to veil His rule and to demonstrate His Lordship's majesty in this life. However, He also has installed a "private telephone" in His servants' hearts so that, leaving all means and causes behind, they can contact Him and declare: *You alone do we worship and from You alone do we seek help* (1:5). Phrases like *the Best of Creators, the Most Merciful of the Merciful,* and *God is the Greatest* also underline this fact.

As for how we can judge something as perfect if it has no opposite, consider the following five points:

First point: One who asks such a question is unaware of true perfection and imagines relative perfections to be true. Any virtue, perfection, or superiority that manifests itself in comparison to or in contrast with others is not true; rather, it is of relative value and significance. Thus losing its opposite causes it to lose its value.

For example, heat is desired over severe cold and food is delicious in proportion to one's hunger. Without cold and hunger, heat and food have no value. True pleasure, love, perfection, or virtue do not show themselves in comparison with others or in proportion to their opposites' degree—they are by and of themselves, and so are realities unto themselves.

Life contains realities that do not need comparisons or opposites to perceive or appreciate: the pleasure of existing, life, mercy, compassion, belief, love, knowledge, and life's continuance; the beauty of light, countenance, moral virtues, and good conduct; the delight and beauty of seeing and hearing; and the perfection of Divine Essence, Attributes, and acts, which do not change. With or without opposites, they are virtues and perfections in themselves. Thus all perfections of the Majestic Maker, the Author of Grace and Beauty, and the Creator of Perfection are true in and of themselves. The perfections in creation are their reflections according to the capacity of each being.

Second point: In *Sharh al-Mawaqif*, Sayed Sharif al-Jurjani writes: "Love is caused by pleasure, benefit, sexual or natural inclination, or perfection. Perfection is loved because of itself." In other words, you love something or someone due to the resulting pleasure or benefit, your sexual or natural (e.g., fatherly, motherly, filial, etc.) inclination, or its perfection. If perfection arouses love, there is no need to search for another cause. For example, people tend to love people of perfection and of perfect virtue although they have no relation to them whatsoever.

So as they are true, indisputable, and infinite, all of Almighty God's perfections and His Most Beautiful Names are loved because of themselves. The Majestic Being, Who is absolutely worthy of love and is the True Beloved One, loves His perfections and the beauties of His Names and Attributes. These are true and exist in a manner suitable to Him. He loves the works of His art, which mirror His perfections, and the beauties of His creatures. He loves His Prophets and saints, particularly His noble beloved, the lord of Messengers and master of saints—Prophet Muhammad.

Due to His love for His Own Beauty, He loves His beloved, who mirrors that Beauty. Due to His love for His Own Names, He loves His beloved, who manifests those Names in a most comprehensive way, as well as all other Prophets. Due to His love for His art, He loves His beloved, who displays that art, and those who are like him (the other Prophets).

Due to His love for His creatures, He loves His beloved, who welcomes those creatures with due appreciation and applause, saying: "What wonders God has willed! God bless them! How beautifully they have been created!" and those who follow him. Due to His love for the beauties of His creatures, He loves His beloved, who is the most comprehensive embodiment of all those beauties and all moral virtues shared by them, and his followers.

Third point: All perfections in the universe are signs of a Majestic One's perfections and indications of His Beauty. In relation to His Perfection, all beauty and perfection is an indistinct shadow. I now present brief pointers to five evidences of this reality.

First evidence: A splendid, perfectly built and decorated palace points to perfect engineering, architecture, and joinery. This perfect engineering, architecture, and joinery point to one worthy of called by such titles as builder, engineer, architect, decorator, and joiner. These titles show the perfection of the builder's artistry, which points to his competence. This perfect competence shows that the builder is a perfect one of a most sublime nature.

Similarly this world, a perfectly built and decorated palace, points to the perfection of acts, for a perfect work results from perfect acts. Perfect acts point to such perfect Names as Organizer, Fashioner, Wise, Decorator, and Builder, which are involved in building the palace. Perfect Names and Titles show perfect qualities or Attributes, for if the latter are imperfect, the Names originating from them also are imperfect.

Perfect Attributes demonstrate perfect competence that, in turn, shows that the One Who built that palace is perfect. Although His Perfection is manifested through the veils of Essential Competence, Attributes, Names, acts, and works, it still reveals the faultless perfection and beauty seen everywhere.

After you see that infinite perfection originating in the Essence of the One Who has it, you may understand how imperfect and dim are the relative perfections manifested in comparison to others or by way of contrast.

Second evidence: When viewed with attentive eyes and considered reflectively, the universe reveals to the heart and sound conscience that the One Who has made it so beautiful and decked it out with such varieties of adornment has such infinite beauty and perfection that He has made it so.

Third evidence: Perfect and well-proportioned works of art depend on perfect planning that, in turn, is based on comprehensive knowledge, a productive mind, intellectual refinement, and spiritual purity. The spirit's purity shows itself in the work through knowledge. So, with all its material beauties, this universe consists of the drops issuing from an infinite knowledge belonging to One Who has infinite beauty and perfection.

Fourth evidence: As you know, a being of light diffuses light and illuminates, and benevolence coming from wealth and grace originates from a gracious one. Since this is so, like light pointing to the sun, all the beauty and perfection observed in the universe point to a perpetual beauty.

Like a mighty river glittering with reflections of the sun's light, creatures flow over Earth's face, glittering with reflections of beauty and perfection. Just as reflections of light in bubbles on a river's surface do not originate from the bubbles themselves, so the beauties and perfections glittering temporarily on the flood of creatures do not belong to the creatures themselves; rather, they are reflections of the lights of an Eternal Sun's Names.

The disappearance of mirrors and the death of creatures, in contrast to the perpetual reflections in them of inseparable grace and beauty, are among the most manifest proofs that apparent beauty does not belong to those reflecting them, and that there is One with ideal beauty and ever-manifested kindness and grace, One Whose existence is absolutely necessary, Who is Eternal and All-Loving.

Fifth evidence: If several people coming from the same place through different ways report the same event, it means that the event occurred. In the same way, all people who can uncover hidden truths and are as sure of them as if they had seen them with their own eyes, whether truth-seeking purified scholars, saints belonging to different spiritual orders, or sages belonging to different schools of thought, regardless of time, place, or capacity, have agreed that the beauties and perfections seen in the mirrors of the universe's creatures are reflections of the Perfection of a Single Necessarily Existent One and manifestations of the beauty of His Names. This consensus is an unshakable and decisive testimony.

Fourth point: A person's or a thing's pleasure or beauty are judged according to those who receive and manifest them, not according to their opposites. For example, generosity is a beautiful and praiseworthy virtue. Generous people receive far greater pleasure from the happiness of those whom they have favored than from their superiority to others in generosity.

Caring and compassionate people feel greater pleasure in proportion to the comfort of those for whom they feel compassion. For example, a mother's compassion for her children causes her to have such a great and strong pleasure in her children's happiness and well-being that she nearly sacrifices her life for them. Such a pleasure also causes a hen to attack a dog to protect her young.

True pleasure, beauty, and perfection of laudable virtues and praiseworthy qualities are judged according to that with which they are related, not to their likes or opposites. Given this, the Beauty of the Perfect and All-Gracious One's Mercy, the All-Living, Self-Subsistent, All-Benevolent, All-Caring, All-Merciful, and All-Compassionate should be considered in view of those toward whom He has mercy.

According to the degree of happiness and well-being of those whom He favors with His Mercy, particularly their enjoyment of His bounties in Paradise, the All-Merciful and All-Compassionate One feels what we call sacred love, sacred pleasure, sacred exhilaration, and sacred joy. All of these accord with His Holy, Transcendent Being, and are infinitely greater, as well as more sacred, elevated, and refined, than their counterparts in creation.

You may see one manifestation of this mighty truth's comprehensive meaning via the following comparison: Suppose a kind, compassionate, and generous man wills to feed some very poor, hungry, and destitute people. So, he prepares a banquet on his fine ship and watches them from above while they eat. You may understand how much their enjoyment of the food in gratitude and their happiness in praise and thankfulness please and exhilarate that noble and generous person.

Similarly, the All-Merciful and Compassionate One has spread out a vast food-laden table on Earth's face and causes Earth to travel in the space with all of its inhabitants. He feeds them from the food on this table and invites those of His servants who are infinitely hungry and destitute to Paradise's everlasting gardens. He prepares each garden as if it were a magnificent table laid out with all kinds of food and drink, which are of pure pleasure and delight. Consider the pleasure and happiness that the above-mentioned person feels at his guests' enjoyment, although he is not the true owner of what he offers, and then compare it with the indescribable sacred love and pleasure felt by the All-Merciful One.

Consider this. If a skillful technician invents something that works as intended, he or she will be pleased and say: "What wonders God has willed." The Majestic Maker has invented the vast universe. He has made Earth (in general) and each creature in it (in particular), especially our head, in such a way that science should be lost in admiration. Each creature displays the expected results to the utmost degree and in a very beautiful way. Their obedience to God's laws for the universe's creation and operation, which comprise their worship, glorification, and specific praise and exaltation of Him, as well as the attainment of Divine purposes for their lives, please Him to a degree beyond our comprehension.

Or, say a just judge receives great pleasure from doing and establishing justice, and becomes extremely happy when able to restore the rights of the oppressed. Compare with this the sacred meanings arising from the reality that the Absolutely Just Ruler, the Majestic Overwhelming One, gives all creatures the right of existence. He gives animate beings the right of life, protects and maintains their existence and lives against aggression, restores all rights in the universe, acts with absolute justice, and will judge humanity and jinn in the Hereafter and establish absolute justice.

As in the examples above, each Divine Name contains many sorts of beauty, grace, and perfection, as well as many levels of love, pride, honor, and grandeur. This is why exacting saintly scholars, who manifest the Divine Name the All-Loving, have concluded: "The essence of the universe is love. All creatures move with the motive of love. All laws of attraction, rapture, and gravity originate in love." One of them even said:

> The spheres are intoxicated,
> angels are intoxicated, and so are stars.
> The heavens, the sun, the moon,
> and Earth are intoxicated.
> Intoxicated are the elements and plants

> and trees and human beings.
> All animate beings are intoxicated,
> and so are all atoms of creation.

Every creature is intoxicated, according to its capacity, with the "wine" of Divine love. People love those who are kind to them as well as true perfection and transcendent beauty. They also love those who are kind to those whom they love and for whom they have mercy.

Given this, we can understand that the Majestic and Beautiful, the Most Beloved of Perfection, in each of Whose Names are innumerable treasuries of kindness, Who makes all those whom we love happy with His favors and is the source of countless perfections and levels of beauty and grace, is worthy of infinite love and the creation's intoxication with His love. This is why some saints who have manifested the Divine Name the All-Loving have said: "We do not even want Paradise. One gleam of the Divine love is eternally sufficient for us," and why, as Prophet Muhammad said: "One minute spent in beholding the Divine Beauty in Paradise excels all the bounties of Paradise."

So, perfect love and perfections attained through love are possible within the spheres of the universal manifestations of Divine Names on beings as a whole (Unity) and the spheres of their particular manifestations on individuals (Oneness or Uniqueness). Any perfections imagined outside those spheres are false.

Fifth point: The representative of the misguided says: "Your Traditions condemn the world, describing it as flesh. All people of truth and sainthood deplore it, considering it evil and foul. But you say it is the means for showing all Divine perfections, and speak of it like a lover."

Answer: The world has three facets. The first facet is concerned with Almighty God's Names and shows their inscriptions and functions as mirrors to them. This facet is the Eternally-Besought-of-All's collection of innumerable "letters." Therefore it is extremely beautiful and worthy of love. The second facet relates to the Hereafter. It is the field to sow for the Hereafter, the tillage of Paradise, the flowerbed of Divine Mercy. Like the first one, it is beautiful and worthy of love.

The third facet is a veil of heedlessness, a plaything for human fancy and desire. It is ugly because it is mortal, painful, and deceptive, and thus condemned by the Traditions and disliked by the people of truth. The Qur'an praises creation and attaches importance to its first two facets. The Companions and saints sought those facets.

Four groups of people condemn and deplore the world. The first group, those with knowledge of God, condemn it because it builds a barrier in front of the knowledge, love, and worship of Almighty God. The second group consists of those who aim solely at the Hereafter. They abhor the world because its affairs and occupations prevent them from striving for the Hereafter seriously, or because their firm belief and conviction show it to be very ugly when compared with Paradise's beauties and perfections. Just as all men are ugly when compared with Prophet Joseph, all the world's beauties and charms mean nothing when compared with those of Paradise.

The third group, those who cannot conquer the world, condemn it out of their love for—not their dislike of—the world. The fourth group condemns the world because whatever its members grasp slips out of their grasp. They become angry and console themselves by declaring the world ugly. Such condemnation also arises from love of the world. Agreeable condemnation comes from those who love the Hereafter and knowledge of God.

For the sake of the Master of Messengers, may Almighty God include us among the first two groups. Amen.

Third station

In the Name of God,
the Merciful, the Compassionate.

There is nothing that does not glorify Him with praise.

This Third Station consists of two topics.

FIRST TOPIC: According to the meaning of *There is nothing that does not glorify Him with praise,* everything has many aspects, like windows, opened on Almighty God. All truths contained in creation are based on the Divine Names. Each thing owes its existence and essential nature to one or several of God's Names. The variety of art in things and the sciences also are based on a Divine Name. For example, philosophy, in its true sense, depends on the Name All-Wise, medicine on the Name All-Healing, and geometry and engineering are based on the Names All-Determining, All-Proportioning, and All-Giving of Exact Measure.

All human arts and levels of human perfections have their sources in Divine Names. Some exacting saintly scholars have concluded: "A thing's reality consists in Divine Names, and its nature is the inscription of those realities. The manifestations of 20 Divine Names can be seen in one living creature." We will discuss this subtle and comprehensive truth through a comparison and an analysis.

When extremely skillful sculptors want to draw a beautiful flower and sculpt a beautiful woman, they first determine the general lines and then, basing themselves on exact measures and planning, pursue their goals by using the necessary engineering or design knowledge. With the compasses of knowledge and purpose (or wisdom), they draw the outer lines of the eyes, ears, and the nose, and the leaves and seed-producing parts in a proportionate manner, thereby displaying their art and accord with the parts' actual functions. This shows that these sculptors are great artists who do everything for a purpose and put everything in its proper place.

Each sculptor attaches great importance to the work's beauty and adornment, which greatly contributes to his or her art. As these sculptors are benevolent and want to see everybody happy, their works give the impression of pleasure and happiness, which, in turn, suggest that the sculptors are kind and gracious. These attributes originate from their love of beings. As the sculptors want other beings to recognize and love them so that they might ask for help, a desire arising from the sculptors' compassion and desire to benefit others, they fill the woman's arms with everything beneficial and attach jewels to the flower.

The sculptors' personal perfections and virtues cause compassion and tenderness for others to arise in them, and they unite beauty and love in themselves. Since their sublime feelings are so pure that they become happy and exhilarated only when they see others happy, they want to be known by others. Thus they make pictures and statues that reflect all their virtues and laudable qualities.

Similarly, the All-Wise Maker has created Paradise and the world, the heavens and Earth, animals, jinn and humanity, and angels and spirit beings by manifesting His Names. He determines each according to certain measures and gives each a certain form. This displays His Names the All-Fashioner, All-Determining, and Giver of

Measure. Fashioning, determining, and giving of measure are based on Knowledge and Wisdom, and therefore point to the Divine Names the All-Knowing and All-Wise.

By displaying His Names the All-Munificent and All-Gracious, He equips His creatures with all necessary well-proportioned parts and gives each part many complex functions. By manifesting the same Names, He furnishes and adorns Earth with minerals, plants, and animals, and also provides Paradise with gardens, palaces, and houses, each of which has a particular beauty and functions.

The All-Wise Creator equips His creatures with the results of showing His Names the All-Munificent and All-Gracious, as if each embodied munificence, grace, and adornment. What leads His Munificence and Graciousness to such a display is His love of creatures and His will to be known by animate beings and loved by conscious ones. Thus the Names the All-Munificent and All-Gracious exhibit the Names the All-Loving and Recognized or Known One.

He adorns all creatures with delicious fruits and the lovely benefits therefrom, bestowing on them all kinds of bounties. This points to the

Names the Giver of Bounties and All-Compassionate, and shows their manifestations from behind apparent veils. His will to show His Mercy and Affection leads the One Who is independent of creation to show His Munificence and Compassion, which causes creatures to recite the Names the All-Merciful and All-Affectionate. His Essential Beauty and Perfection stimulate Him to manifest His Mercy and Affection, to show the Names the All-Beautiful with the All-Loving and All-Compassionate, which are contained in It. Absolute beauty is loved for itself, and the One with absolute beauty loves Himself. Therefore it is both beauty and love. This is also true with perfection, which is loved for itself and not because of anything else. Therefore it is both lover and beloved.

Since a beauty of infinite perfection and a perfection of infinite beauty are loved to an infinite degree, they wish to manifest themselves in mirrors according to the mirror's capacity. As the Essential Beauty and Perfection of the Majestic Maker, the All-Wise One of Beauty, the All-Powerful One of Perfection, will to show mercy and affection, the Names the All-Merciful and All-Caring must manifest themselves. Since the will to show mercy and affection is associated with compassion and bountifulness, it urges the Names the All-Compassionate and Giver of Bounties to be manifested. Compassion and bountifulness require and cause the Names the All-Loving and the Recognized to manifest themselves.

Being loved and recognized incite manifestations of grace and munificence and cause creatures to show the Names the All-Gracious One and the Munificent One. Grace and munificence incite the Names the All-Decorating and All-Illuminating and show their acts via the beauty and illumination seen in creatures. Decoration and illumination require manifestations of the Names the Maker and the Benevolent and demonstrate them via all creatures' beautiful countenances. Making and benevolence are based on knowledge and wisdom and show the Names the All-Knowing and All-Wise via all creatures' harmonious and purposeful organization. Demanding acts of organizing, fashioning and forming, as well as of knowledge and wisdom, show the Names the Fashioner and Giver of Measure via all creatures' general forms.

In short, the Majestic Maker has made all creatures in such a way that most of them, particularly animate ones, display most of the Divine Names. It is as if He clothed each creature in 20 different garments, one over the other, and inscribed several of His Names on each one. For example, as pointed out in the above comparison, there are many layers of loveliness in the apparent creation of a beautiful flower and a beautiful woman. Compare vast and universal bodies with these two particular examples.

FIRST LAYER: Their general forms and appearances, which recite: "O Fashioner, O Giver of Measure, O Determiner, O Organizer."

SECOND LAYER: Their form and appearance, including all bodily members and parts, that show many Names like the All-Knowing and All-Wise.

THIRD LAYER: The forms of beauty and adornment particular to each bodily member and part, on which are inscribed many Names like the Maker and the One Who Creates Subtly and Perfectly.

FOURTH LAYER: The detail of ornament, beauty, and elegance given to creatures as if in the embodied form of grace and munificence. They recite: "O Gracious One, O Munificent One," and many other Names.

Fifth layer: The delicious fruits attached to that flower and lovely children, as well as the laudable virtues given to that woman as gifts, show Names like the All-Loving, All-Compassionate, and Giver of Bounties.

Sixth layer: This layer of bountifulness and benevolence recites: "O All-Merciful, O All-Caring," and several other Names.

Seventh layer: The bounties given to them and the results attached to their existence show such gleams of beauty and grace that they deserve pure gratitude and love kneaded with true eagerness and tenderness. This layer manifests such Names as the All-Beautiful One of Perfection and the Perfect One of Beauty.

If a flower and a beautiful woman display so many Names through their outward forms, you may compare how many Names of universal manifestation all flowers, animate beings, and vast and universal bodies demonstrate. You may understand how many sacred, enlightening Names of God (e.g., the All-Living, Self-Subsistent, and Giver of Life) a person manifests through his or her spirit, heart, reason, life, and all other senses and faculties.

Paradise, the community of houris, Earth's face, and springtime are all flowers. Heaven is a flower; the stars are its gilded embroideries. The sun is a flower; the seven colors in its light are its dyes. The cosmos is a beautiful, macro-human being; humanity is a normo-universe. Houris, spirit beings, angels, jinn, and humanity have been fashioned, organized, and created as if they were beautiful individuals. As they collectively and individually manifest the All-Majestic Being's Names, each one is a different mirror to His Beauty, Perfection, Mercy, and Love. Each is also a different and true witness, as well as a different sign, of His Infinite Beauty, Perfection, Mercy, and Love. As all boundless perfections are possible only in the sphere of Divine Unity and Oneness or Uniqueness, any perfections imagined outside of this sphere are false.

The realities of things are based on the Divine Names, or rather they are manifestations of those Names. All things mention their Maker in numerous tongues. Also, know one of the meanings of "There is nothing that does not glorify Him with praise." Say: "Glory be to Him Who is veiled through His manifestation's intensity." Understand the reason why He is the All-Mighty, All-

Wise; He is All-Forgiving, All-Compassionate; He is All-Knowing, All-Powerful," and similar phrases repeated at the end of Qur'anic verses.

If you cannot see clearly the Names displayed on a flower, ponder on Paradise, look at spring attentively, or examine Earth's face. You can read clearly the Names inscribed in those huge flowers of Mercy and see the Names' distinct manifestations.

SECOND TOPIC: Left without any support, the representative of the misguided reveals his or her real intention: "Since I find worldly pleasure, happiness, and advancement in civilization in denying God and the Hereafter, in loving this world, and in human freedom and self-confidence, I bring others to this path, with Satan's help, and will continue to do so."

ANSWER: I say in the Qur'an's name: O helpless one, come to your senses and don't listen to this misguided follow. If you do, you will lose. There are two paths before you: the one offered by the misguided and that described in the Qur'an. The misguided and the dissolute, who associate partners with God and transgress Divine Commands, fall to bottomless depths of degradation. They place an unbearable load on their weak backs and burden their hearts with boundless sorrow.

If they do not recognize and place their trust in Almighty God, they become like very weak, impotent, infinitely poor, and destitute animals, or mortal beings afflicted with pain and grief, subject to countless calamities. They suffer incessantly, for they remain separated from all things and people that they have loved and to which they have been connected. Leaving all things and people amidst the pain of separation, they enter the grave's dark depths alone.

They struggle in vain, with a limited will, little power, a short life-span, and a dull mind against infinite pain and ambition. They strive to realize their countless desires and goals, but without any considerable result. While they cannot bear even the burden of their own being, they load their minds and backs with the burden of the world. They suffer Hell's torments even before reaching it.

To endure such a painful spiritual torment, they seek out heedlessness as a kind of anesthesia. But they begin to feel this pain most acutely as they approach the grave. Not being true servants of Almighty God, they believe that they own themselves. In reality, however, they cannot govern their being in this tumultuous world, for they have only limited free will, insignificant power, and many enemies ready to attack. They look at the grave in fear and terror.

As human beings, they are related to humanity and the world. But since they deny that the world and humanity belong to the One Who is All-Wise, All-Knowing, All-Powerful, All-Compassionate, and All-Munificent, they attribute their existence and lives to chance and nature. And so the world's fearful events (e.g., convulsions, earthquakes, plagues, calamity, death, and famine) and humanity's conditions and experiences always trouble them. Moreover, they must contend with their own pain and the troubles that other creatures cause them to suffer.

As their own disbelief brought them to this deplorable state, how can they deserve mercy and affection? This reminds us of The Eighth Word's parable of two brothers who fell into two wells. Those who are not content with a fine banquet's agreeable and lawful enjoyment and entertainment, or with honest friends and in a beautiful garden, bring trouble upon themselves. Drinking wine to obtain an unlawful pleasure, they imagine themselves surrounded by wild beasts in a dirty place on a winter day and so tremble and cry in fear.

Do such people deserve pity? Seeing their honest friends as wild beasts, they insult them. They see delicious food as foul; clean, fine plates and bowls as worthless, dirty stones; and attempt to break them. Moreover, they judge the invaluable, meaningful books that they are to read and study as ordinary, meaningless collections of sheets, and tear them up and scatter them. Such people deserve to be punished.

Unbelief and misguidance arise from abusing one's willpower. Such people assert that the All-Wise Maker's guest-house of the world is a plaything of chance and nature and that the transference of beings to the World of the Unseen, after completing their duty of refreshing the Divine Names' manifestations, is going into absolute non-existence.

They commit many other acts worthy of punishment, such as judging beings' glorifications and recitations of the Divine Names as outcries of death and eternal separation; sheets of creatures, each a missive of the Eternally-Besought-of-All, to be confused, meaningless collections; the grave's door, which opens onto the World of Mercy, as opening onto a dark world of non-existence; and death as separation from—not reunion with—all friends and beloved ones. In such ways do they deliver themselves to a very painful punishment. Since they deny, reject, and insult all creatures, the Divine Names, and His inscriptions and missives, they deserve punishment.

So, unfortunate people of misguidance and dissipation, can any of your progress, evolution, science, technology, and civilization compensate for such a terrible loss, collapse, and crushing hopelessness? Where is the true consolation that the human spirit urgently needs above all else? What nature or causality, what thing upon which you rely and to which you attribute His works, bounties, and favors, can help you after death?

Which of your discoveries, inventions, idols, and fetishes can save you from the darkness of death, which you suppose to be eternal extinction? Which one can take you through the Intermediate World of the grave, the Plain of Resurrection and Gathering, and over the Bridge to the Abode of Eternal Happiness? Since you cannot close the grave's door, you are bound to traverse and tread this way (passing through the stations mentioned.) To travel it safely, you must depend on the One Who commands and controls all those worlds and abodes.

O unfortunate, misguided, and heedless people. Misusing the potential of loving and knowing given to you to know and love God and His Attributes and Names, you love your selves and the world. This, as well as your similar misuse of your body and faculties that were given so that you could worship and thank Him, causes you to suffer deserved punishment. Assigning to your selves the love that must be felt for Almighty God, you suffer the resulting troubles. All this is because any love directed to other than that which deserves it brings suffering. You do not provide true peace and happiness for what you adore: your carnal self. Since you do not submit and entrust it to the Absolutely Powerful One, the True Beloved One, you always suffer pain.

Since you assign the love belonging to Almighty God's Names and Attributes to the world and attribute the works of His art to causality and nature, you have no right to complain. That which you love either leaves you without saying good-bye or does not recognize you. Even if it recognizes you, it does not love you. Even if it loves you, it gives you no benefit. You suffer from incessant separation and death without hope of reunion.

This is the reality of what such people call the happiness of life and human perfection, beauty of civilization, and pleasure of freedom. Dissipation and drunkenness temporarily veil the suffering and pain that eventually will come upon them. In contrast, the Qur'an's light-diffusing way heals the wounds afflicting the misguided with the truths of belief, disperses the darkness enveloping them, and closes the doors of misguidance and waste.

This way removes our weakness, impotence, poverty, and need, for it enables us to trust in an All-Powerful One of Compassion. Submitting the burden of being and life to His Power and Mercy, we transform the self and life into a mount. We learn that we are true human beings and the All-Merciful One's welcomed guests. Showing the world as the All-Merciful One's guest-house, its creatures as mirrors of Divine Names and ever-recruited missives of the Eternally-Besought-of-All, it heals perfectly all wounds caused by transience, decay, and impermanent love. It also saves us from the darkness of whims and fancies. Showing life as the prelude to reunion with deceased friends and beloved ones, it heals the wounds of death, which the misguided regard as eternal separation, and shows that separation is actually reunion.

By showing that the grave is a door opened onto the World of Mercy, the Abode of Happiness, the gardens of Paradise, and the luminous Realm of the All-Merciful One, the way of the Qur'an removes our greatest fear. It causes us to understand that our journey in the Intermediate World, which seems to be most depressing and troublesome, is really most pleasant and exhilarating. It demonstrates that the grave is not like a dragon's mouth, but rather a door opened onto the gardens of Divine Mercy. It informs believers:

> Your willpower is very limited, so entrust your affairs to your Owner's universal Will. Your power is slight and insignificant, so rely on the Absolutely

Powerful One's Power. Your life is short, so consider eternal life. Your mind is dull, so come into the Qur'an's sun. Look at it with the light of belief, so that in place of your mind, which gives light like a firefly, each Qur'anic verse gives you light like a star. If you have endless ambition and pain, boundless reward and infinite mercy await you. If you have limitless desire and aims, do not be anxious, for you cannot realize all of them here. This is only possible in another realm, and the One Who gives them to you is not your self.

And:

You do not own yourself, but are owned by One infinitely Powerful and an infinitely Compassionate One of Majesty. Do not trouble yourself by placing your being and life on your shoulders, for the One Who has given and governs your life is He. The world's Owner is the All-Wise and All-Knowing. Whatever He does is done out of compassion. In many respects, even His wrath is based on His Compassion. You are His guest in His world, so do not interfere with what is beyond your power and responsibility. Such living beings like humanity and animals are not left to themselves.

> Rather, they are officials charged with certain duties and are controlled and favored by an All-Compassionate Ruler, Who has preferred them over most of His creatures. He has far more compassion for them than for you. Furthermore, all things and events that appear hostile to you are controlled and governed by that All-Compassionate Ruler. He is the All-Wise and so does nothing useless, and the All-Compassionate Whose every act contains a kind of grace.

It adds:

> This transient world provides the necessities of the afterlife. It decays, but yields everlasting fruits and displays a Permanent One's Eternal Names. In return for its few pleasures, it causes one to suffer many pains and afflictions. However, the favors of the All-Merciful, All-Compassionate One are true and lasting pleasures, and its pains cause one to obtain many spiritual rewards. What is lawful is sufficient for the spirit's enjoyment and pleasures, as well as for the heart and carnal self, so do not enter upon what is unlawful. Any illicit pleasure results in numerous pains and causes one to lose the All-Merciful One's favors, which are pure, lasting pleasures.

Misguidance so debases humanity that no philosophic trend, scientific development, or human civilization and progress can lift people out of that deep pit of darkness. Through belief and righteous deeds, the wise Qur'an takes us out of the lowest pit and raises us to the highest rank. It fills that deep pit with the steps of spiritual progress and the means of spiritual perfection.

The Qur'an facilitates our long, troubling, and stormy journey toward eternity. It shows us how to traverse in a day the distance that normally takes 50,000 years to cover. By enabling us to know the majestic Being, the King of Eternity and uncontained by time and space, it honors us with being His dutiful servants and guests and secures for us an easy and comfortable journey through the world and through the mansions of the Intermediate World of the grave and the Hereafter.

A king's righteous, dutiful officials travel in his domain in security, via the fastest modes of transportation, and easily cross provincial boundaries. In the same way, those connected with the Eternal King through belief, as well as those who show obedience to Him through righteous deeds, travel through the stations and across the boundaries of the world and the realms of the grave and the Hereafter with the speed of lightning or Buraq, the mount of Paradise. Such people find eternal happiness. The Qur'an proves the truth of this, and purified religious scholars and saints see it clearly.

The Qur'an also says:

O believers, do not waste your God-given infinite capacity of loving on your ugly, defective, evil, and harmful carnal self. Do not adore it or follow its desires and fancies as if it were an object of worship, but direct it toward the One worthy of infinite love, Who does you infinite good and will make you infinitely happy; Who through His favors makes happy those with whom you have connections and whose happiness pleases you; One with infinite perfection and infinitely sacred, transcendent, pure, perfect, and undecaying beauty; Whose every Name radiates numerous lights of beauty and grace; the beauty of Whose Mercy and the mercy of Whose Beauty are displayed in Paradise; and Whose Beauty and Perfection point to and are signs of all the beauty, grace, and perfection in the universe, which are lovable. Love Him, and make Him the sole object of your worship.

Furthermore it says:

O humanity, do not use your infinite capacity of loving, which has been given to you to love His Names and Attributes, to love impermanent beings. All that exists, except for Him, is transitory, whereas the Divine Beautiful Names displayed on mortals are permanent and constant. Each Name and Attribute has thousands of degrees of favoring and thousands of levels of perfection and love. Consider, for example, the Name the All-Merciful: Paradise is one of its manifestations, eternal happiness is one of its radiances, and all provisions and bounties bestowed on worldly creatures are just one of its drops.

To see how the Qur'an expresses the difference between these two ways, consider: *We have created humanity in the fairest form and the best pattern of creation. Then We have returned it to the lowest of the low, except those who believe and do righteous deeds* (95:4-6) and *Neither the heavens nor Earth wept over their destruction* (44:29). See in what elevated and miraculous style they express the difference! A detailed explanation of the first verse can be found in The Eleventh Word. Here we present a few remarks on the exalted truth contained in the other verse, which explicitly states that the heavens and Earth do not weep when unbelievers die. This implies that the heavens and Earth weep when believers die.

Unbelievers do not know the meaning of the heavens and Earth, do not recognize their Maker, deny their duties, and so reduce their value. Such insults and hostility cause the heavens and Earth to be pleased when such people die. But they weep when believers die, for believers know the duties of the heavens and Earth and affirm the reality they bear. As their belief enlightens them about these meanings, they say: "How beautifully they have been created. How well they perform their duties." Believers acknowledge their value and respect them accordingly. They also love them and the Names to which they are mirrors in Almighty God's name. And so the heavens and Earth grieve for them.

AN IMPORTANT QUESTION: Loving is not voluntary. I have a natural need to love delicious foods and fruits, my parents and children, my spouse and friends, virtuous people, life, youth, this world, spring, and beautiful things. Why should I not? How can I appropriate all such instances of love only to the Divine Being and His Names and Attributes?

ANSWER: Listen to the following four subtle points.

FIRST SUBTLE POINT: However involuntary loving is, you can direct it to a certain object. For example, by convincing yourself that something beloved is ugly, or an obstacle to or only a mirror for an object worthy of true love, this feeling of love can be diverted to the true object of love.

SECOND SUBTLE POINT: You can love such things, but do so in Almighty God's name and for His love's sake. Loving delicious foods and fruits because they are favors and bounties of Almighty God, the All-Merciful and All-Compassionate, means loving the Names the All-Merciful and Giver of Bounties and is a sort of thanksgiving. Love, when done in the All-Merciful One's name and not the carnal self's name, is reflected by lawful earning, contentment with what is lawful, and consuming in gratitude and reflection.

Loving and respecting one's parents on behalf of the Mercy and Wisdom that equipped them with affection and tenderness, and that raised you through their compassionate hands, are included in God's love. If done for Almighty God's sake, you must show your parents much more love, respect, and care when they only can cause you difficulty. The verse: *If either or both of them reach old age with you, do not say to them "Uff!"* (17:23), which tells children to love and respect their parents in five ways and degrees, shows how important parents' rights are in the eyes of the Qur'an and how degrading and detestable filial ingratitude is.

Since a father typically prefers his children to be superior to him, children cannot claim rights against him. There can be no justifiable cause of dispute between parents and children, for a dispute arises either from envy or a violation of rights. A father never envies his children, and children cannot claim rights against him. Even if they consider his treatment of them wrong, they cannot rebel. Those who do so, or who annoy him, are cruel and ungrateful.

Loving one's children with utmost care and compassion, as they are the All-Compassionate,

All-Munificent One's gifts, is included in one's love of Almighty God. The sign that such love is for God's sake is to show "becoming patience" at their death and not to wail in despair and rebelliousness against Destiny. One should submit to God, believing that judgment belongs only to Him, and think: "My child was a loveable creature of God whom He placed in my custody. His Wisdom required Him to take the child from me and to a far better place. Even if I have one apparent share in that servant of His, thousands of true shares belong to Him."

Your love for friends, on account of their being believing friends of Almighty God who do good deeds according to the principle of loving for the sake of God, also is included in love of God. In addition, this is true of the love you feel for your spouse, your companion in life, because he or she is a sweet gracious gift of the Divine Mercy. Do not set your heart on his or her transient good looks.

A woman's greatest charm and beauty lie in her lovable good conduct accompanied with the kindness and grace particular to womanhood, and in her elevated, serious, and sincere compassion.

That beauty of compassion and good conduct increase until she dies. It is through the love and respect for her compassion and good conduct that one can observe her rights to the end. If she is loved because of her physical beauty, she is deprived of her rights and the love and respect due to her at a time when she needs them most.

Loving virtuous people like Prophets and saints because they are approved servants of Almighty God, and in His name and for His sake, are included in His love. If you love your life because it is a most valuable capital given by Almighty God to gain eternal life, a treasury containing the faculties with which to acquire all kinds of virtues and perfections, and if you spend it in His service, then this love is included in love of Almighty God, the True Object of Worship. Loving the prime of youth because it is a sweet, fine gift of Almighty God, and thus spending it in His way is a sort of lawful love wedded to gratitude.

Loving nature reflectively, especially in spring, because it is a realm displaying the most beautiful inscriptions of the All-Wise Maker's light-diffusing Names and the most splendid and embellished works of His art, means to love

Almighty God's Names. If you love the world only because it is the field to sow for the Hereafter, the mirror of the Divine Names, the collection of Almighty God's missives, and a temporary guest-house, then this love is also in Almighty God's name—provided you are not under your carnal self's influence.

In short, love the world and its creatures not for themselves but in the name of their Creator and the meaning they contain. Do not say: "How beautiful they are!" Rather, say: "How beautifully they have been made!" In your heart, do not love that which is not Him. Do not set your heart on that which is not Him, for the heart is the Eternally-Besought-of-All's mirror and belongs to Him. So pray to Him: "O God, provide me with love of You and the love of what will make me near to You."

And so if all the types of love mentioned so far are in God's name, then they give a painless, pure pleasure and are the means of a union that does not allow separation. In addition, they cause your love of God to grow and can be considered gratitude that gives pure pleasure and a reflection that is itself pure love.

For example, if a noble king grants you an apple in his presence, you will receive two sorts of pleasure and feel two kinds of love. The first type is your love for the apple because it is an apple. Thus you receive as much pleasure as an apple can give. Such a love is not in the king's name, but arises from your love of yourself, for you love the apple because of the pleasure it gives you. This kind of pleasure is transient and ends when you finish eating the apple. Moreover, the king may not be pleased with such an attitude.

The second sort of pleasure and love are directly related to the king. If you love and respect the apple because it embodies the royal compliment to you, then this love is in the king's name and for his sake. The pleasure arising from such a compliment is far greater than the pleasure coming from eating the apple. Such an attitude is pure gratitude to the king for his gift, and the love shown for the apple is love for the king himself.

Likewise, loving bounties—all foods and fruits—granted to us because of themselves and the pleasure they give is a carnal love, for it is for the carnal self's sake. The pleasure coming from eating and drinking is transient and mixed with pain. If you love the bounties you receive on account of their being favors of Divine Mercy and fruits of Divine Bountifulness and Benevolence, and if you receive pleasure from them and have an appetite for them in appreciation of the Divine grace in them, this love is pure gratitude and pure pleasure without any pain.

THIRD SUBTLE POINT: Love of the Divine Names has degrees and levels. As pointed out above, sometimes you love the Divine Names because you love their works in the universe, because they are titles of Divine perfections, or because you are in limitless need of them due to your comprehensive nature.

For example, while you are seeking help in utter despair for your relatives or for poor, weak, and needy creatures, someone appears unexpectedly and does for them what you wished to do for them. How much would you love such a person for his munificence and benevolence, and always be thankful to him for those qualities? Similarly, consider the Names All-Merciful and All-Compassionate.

By showing these Names, Almighty God favors your believing parents and ancestors, as well as your friends and beloved ones, in this world with all His bounties. Since He will make both you and them happy in Paradise, in the World of Eternal Bliss, through seeing Him and all paradisiacal pleasures and bringing you together, you may understand how much these two Names are worthy of your love, to what extent your spirit needs them, and how proper and necessary it is to say: "All praise be to God for His being the All-Merciful and All-Compassionate."

Also, with its creatures being its amiable residents and lovable adornments, the world is like a home for you. You feel a profound connection with it, and its conditions affect you deeply. Through reflection, you may perceive how much your spirit loves and to what degree you need the Names the All-Wise and All-Sustaining of the One Who has organized the world and it creatures and thus governs, grows, and sustains them with perfect wisdom.

You also may understand to what extent your spirit needs the Names the Heir, All-Quickening, Permanent, Munificent, Giver of Life, and Benevolent of the One Who brings all of the deceased to whom you feel connected, and at whose decay you are grieved, out of the darkness of eternal extinction and settles them in a place far more beautiful than this world.

Since we are noble, elevated beings with comprehensive natures, we need 1,001 Divine Names in many circumstances of destitution. A manifold need is eagerness, a manifold eagerness is love, and a manifold love is adoration. In proportion to the degree of the spirit's perfection, love increases and flourishes in degrees according to the levels of the Divine Names' manifestations. Since the Names are titles with which the Majestic Being shows Himself, love of the Names turns into love of the Divine Being. Out of thousands of levels of manifestations of the Names the Just, All-Wise, Truth, and All-Compassionate, we present one as an example.

If you want to see the Names the All-Merciful, All-Compassionate, and Truth in full manifestation in wisdom and justice, consider the following comparison:

Suppose that each company of a 400-company army has unique uniforms, rations, weaponry, and medicines. If these companies are situated together mixed with one another without the uniqueness of each being considered, and yet, out of his perfect compassion, based on his extraordinary power and miraculously encompassing knowledge, and with utmost justice and wisdom, a peerless king equips each with unique uniforms and weapons and provides them with appropriate foods and medicines without mistake or help, you may understand what a powerful, compassionate, just, and munificent king he is.

In the same way, if you want to see the manifestations of the Divine Names the Truth, Merciful and Compassionate included in the All-Wise and All-Just, you can look at magnificent armies of plants and animals, which consist of countless different families, genera, and species. All of these set up their tents on Earth's face in spring, are mixed with each other, and have unique uniforms, provisions, weaponry, instructions, lifestyles, and demobilizations. Although they have no tongues with which to voice their needs and no power to meet them, see how the One with the Names of Truth, All-Merciful, All-Provider, All-Compassionate, and All-Munificent provides, maintains, and raises them in perfect justice and wisdom, without confusing and forgetting any of them.

Is it possible that another hand could share in this amazing order and all-comprehensive organization based on an absolute measure and balance? Who other than the Unique One of Unity, the Absolutely All-Wise and All-Powerful One, could share in this art, this regulation and government, and this raising and sustaining?

FOURTH SUBTLE POINT: You ask: "What are the uses and results of my love for foods, selfhood, spouse, parents, children, friends, virtuous people, beautiful things like spring and the world if that love must be in line with the Qur'an's commands?"

Answer: It would take a comprehensive book to explain all of the uses and results of such a love. Thus I restrict myself to pointing out briefly its immediate consequences here and its permanent results in the Hereafter.

As explained above, any love in the carnal self's name, like that of worldly, heedless people, causes pain, trouble, and affliction in this world. For example, compassion turns into a painful affliction because you cannot do something. Love becomes a consuming feeling due to separation. Pleasure becomes like a poisonous drink because it is subject to transience. Since such love is not love in Almighty God's name, it will be useless in the Hereafter. Also, it will bring torment if it has driven the lover into illicit dealings.

Question: How does one's love for Prophets and saints become fruitless?

Answer: Love for Prophets and saints, such as that found among Christians who believe in the Trinity, and the Rafidites (a Shi'a sect) who cherish enmity toward almost all Companions due to their love of 'Ali, is fruitless. [Such love is rooted in love for the person loved. As it is not in God's name, it leads to unforgivable excesses in belief. Due to such excesses, Christians deified Jesus and the Rafidites broke from the majority Muslim community.] Any love in God's name and in the Qur'anic manner yields good results in both this world and the Hereafter. I briefly mention its worldly results below:

- Loving delicious foods and fruits in God's name makes them a favor and grace unmixed with pain, an ease that yields pure thankfulness.

- Loving your carnal self leads you to pity so that you will educate it and prevent it from harmful desires and fancies. When you do this successfully, your carnal self cannot take you wherever it wishes and enslave you to its desires. On the contrary, you will mount it and guide it to truth, not drive it to passions.

- Loving your wife is based on her good conduct and her being a mine of compassion and a gift of Divine Mercy. In return, she will love and respect you. As you both age, this mutual love and respect will grow and increase your happiness. Carnal love based on physical beauty is fleeting. When it disappears, so do your mutual good relations.

- Loving your parents for Almighty God's sake is an act of worship and increases as they age. With a most elevated feeling and endeavor, you pray for them to live long so that you may get more rewards because of them and receive a pure spiritual pleasure by respecting them. If you find their existence unbearable when they need you and thus desire their deaths, you have descended to barbarism and will suffer a painful spiritual ailment.

- Loving your children because they are Almighty God's lovable gifts given to you to raise in an agreeable way is a love that brings happiness and blessing. You will not suffer much because of the calamities striking them or wail in despair if they die. Since their Creator is the All-Wise and All-Compassionate, you will conclude: "Since it was better for them to die than to live, Almighty God took them away from me." Thinking that your patience will draw God's Mercy and that He will bring [both of] you together in an Abode of Eternal Happiness, you will be saved from the pains of separation.

- Loving your friends for God's sake means that separation or death will not break the relationship you currently enjoy. You will benefit from this mutual love and spiritual connection. The pleasure of reunion for His sake is lasting. While a second of union for His sake gives the pleasure of a year of union, a year of being together for worldly purposes means a second of union and ends in painful separation.

- Loving virtuous people like the Prophets and saints shows you the Intermediate World of the grave, which appears to the heedless as a dark, frightening solitude, as a mansion illuminated by the existence of those blessed ones. You will not be afraid to go to that world. Rather, you will feel an inclination and eagerness to go there, and the pleasure you receive from your life will not be spoiled. But if you love them as the "civilized" people love famous individuals, you will be grieved at their death, and the thought of their decay and oblivion in the past's "vast grave" will increase your pain. Thinking that you will enter the grave, which causes even the best people to rot away, you will utter sighs of grief and fear death. But if you love in Almighty God's name, you will see the grave as a place of perfect rest after discarding the body, and you will look forward to it in warm anticipation.

- Loving beautiful things in their Maker's name and in a way reminding you of their Creator is a pleasant reflection and will turn your view, which adores beauty, toward the sources of a far more elevated, sacred, and subtler beauty. You will turn from those beautiful works toward the beauty of Divine acts, then to the beauty of Divine Names, and then to the beauty of Divine Attributes and the Majestic

One's matchless beauty. This love is pure pleasure, an act of worship, and a reflection.

- Loving youth because it is a fine blessing of Almighty God, you will spend it in worship and not waste it in dissipation. When you do that, the worship done while you are young yields permanent fruits. Youth disappears, but those fruits remain and protect you from the evil consequences of a youth spent in rebellion and dissipation. When you grow old, you will concentrate even more on worshipping God and deserve more from Divine Mercy. Unlike the heedless, you will not weep or regret your 5 or 10 years of youthful pleasures as you enter the twilight of your life. You will not be like the heedless, who say: "If only my youth would return, I would tell it what old age has made happen to me."

- Loving such exhibits as spring because they are works of Divine art means that the pleasure of observing them does not disappear when they are removed, for you can recall the meanings they have left in your mind like gilded letters. Like movie scenes, your imagination and time enable you to take pleasure in seeing them, and your mind refreshes the beauties and meanings of the past spring. In such a case, your love continues to give pleasure and enjoyment and does not become painful and temporary.

- Loving this world in Almighty God's name makes all of its creatures like amiable friends. Seeing it as a tillage for the Hereafter, you find in everything a capital that can be used for the good of your afterlife. Calamity does not scare you, and the transience of your life does not trouble you. You will stay in that guest-house peacefully until your appointed hour. But if you love the world as the heedless do, you will suffocate in a troublesome, calamitous, transient, and fruitless love.

If, after indicating the pleasures and benefits that the kind of love taught in the Qur'an will give here, you want to hear and know such love's otherworldly results, read the introduction and nine indications that follow:

Introduction: Through His Majestic Divinity, gracious Mercy, tremendous Lordship, generous Caring, vast Power, and subtle Wisdom, Almighty God has equipped the insignificant-sized human body with so many senses and feelings, such a variety of organs and members and systems, and numerous faculties so that He may make each one of us sense and know the innumerable varieties of His bounties, kinds of His favors, and instances of His Mercy. Also, He has done this so that we can measure and love His Names' countless manifestations. Each bodily member, system, and faculty has different types of service and worship as well as different sorts of pleasures, pains, duties, and rewards.

For example, eyes see the beauties of forms and various miracles of Divine Power in the sphere of sight. Their duty is thoughtful and contemplative observation and gratitude to the Maker. Ears perceive different sounds, creation's sweet melodies, and the subtleties of Divine Mercy in the sphere of hearing. They have their own unique type of worship, pleasure, and reward. The sense of smell is aware of Mercy's subtleties in the sphere of smelling, and also has its own unique pleasure, duty of gratitude, and reward. Like the others, the sense of taste performs many duties of thanksgiving by being aware of the tastes of everything consumed.

In short, all of our senses, organs, and faculties (e.g., the heart, intellect, and spirit) have unique duties, pleasures, and pains. Almighty God, the Absolutely All-Wise One, will reward all of them accordingly. Their reward is either stated explicitly or alluded to in the Qur'an, the truest word, the most perfect system, the Word of God, Who is Sovereign, Mighty, and All-Knowing.

First indication: Lawful love in gratitude for delicious foods and fruits yields paradisiacal foods and fruits in the Hereafter and arouses in us an appetite for them. Even saying: "All praise be to God" after you eat something will be returned to you as a fruit of Paradise. As suggested by the Qur'an and required by Divine Wisdom and Mercy, any pleasurable thanks given to Almighty God for His bounties and favors will be returned to you in Paradise as the most delicious food.

Second indication: In return for loving your selfhood in a lawful manner (pitying it and working to perfect it), you will be given that which you love in Paradise. Since you gratified your selfhood's desires and ambitions and used its organs and faculties in the way Almighty God approves of while here, the Absolutely Munificent One will reward your (lawful) love of it by clothing you in 70 different celestial garments as samples of 70 different kinds of beauty and adornment of Paradise. These will please all of your senses.

He will adorn your body with 70 varieties of beauty and present the houris to you, each of whom is like an animate Paradise. Your love for youth in the world, which shows itself in your using it to worship God, will result in eternal youth in the Abode of Eternal Happiness.

Third indication: In reward for the sincere love you feel for your wife due to her delightful compassion, laudable virtues and good conduct, and protecting her against disobedience to God and other sins, the Absolutely Compassionate One will make her an immortal friend for you in the Abode of Eternal Happiness. She will be more beautiful, better dressed and ornamented, and more charming than the houris. Spouses will be seated on thrones face to face and will take great pleasure in relating to each other their worldly lives they spent together.

Fourth indication: As the result of lawful love for parents and children, Almighty God, the All-Merciful and All-Compassionate, will allow them to come together in Paradise and reward them with eternal happy communion, even though the rank and place of each may be different. He will re-create children who died before puberty as the lovable and most beautiful immortal children of Paradise (56:17), in a form worthy of Paradise, and return them to their parents' arms so that they may enjoy eternally the pleasure of parenthood.

Since Paradise is not the place of reproduction, some thought that the pleasure of having children would be absent there. But as Paradise contains every pleasurable thing in its highest degree, the pleasure of having children, at its best, will be there by means of the children who died before reaching puberty. This is a good tiding for those parents whose prepubescent children have died.

Fifth indication: The Qur'an explicitly states that, as the result of loving righteous friends for God's sake, they will be seated on couches face to face in Paradise and will enjoy eternally the pure pleasure of talking to each other about their worldly lives in a most delightful manner.

Sixth indication: Your Qur'anic love for the Prophets and saints will cause you to benefit from their intercession in the Intermediate World of the grave and in the Plain of Supreme Gathering. You also will receive enlightenment from their elevated positions. According to the rule that "One will be with whom he or she loves," each believer can have a part in the highest rank or position through closeness to the one with that position.

Seventh indication: Your love for beautiful things and spring, expressed in seeing them as the Creator's beautiful works, as well as in appreciating the beauty and harmony of the acts behind those works, the displays of the Names behind those acts, and the displays of the Attributes behind those beautiful Names, will cause you to behold, in the World of Permanence, the displays of those Names, which are far more beautiful than their counterparts in this world, and witness His Beauty and Attributes in those Names. Imam Rabbani says: "Paradise's beauties and subtleties embody the Divine Names' manifestations." Reflect upon these words.

Eighth indication: Your reflective love for this world, on account of its being the Hereafter's tillage and the Divine Names' mirror, will be rewarded with an everlasting garden of Paradise as large as the world. Only the shadowy displays of the Names from behind numerous veils result in the world's amazing beauties. In Paradise, the Names will manifest themselves in a most splendid form. God will give Paradise, in relationship to which this world is like a small seedbed, to those who loved this world as the afterlife's tillage. Also, as required by Mercy and Wisdom and pointed to in the Prophetic Traditions and some Qur'anic verses, our senses and feelings, which are like small shoots here, will be perfected there; our potentials, which are like seeds here, will develop into varieties of perfection and pure pleasure there.

Since we loved the world only in its two aspects concerned with the Hereafter and the Divine Names and not in its contemptible aspect (the cause of all errors), and caused it to prosper through our worship as if we had spent our lives and body, senses, and faculties in worship, Mercy and Wisdom require that we receive a reward as great as the world. Since we loved the Hereafter's tillage for the sake of loving the Hereafter and loved the mirrors of Almighty God's Names for His sake, we will be rewarded with a world-like object of love—a garden of Paradise as vast as the world.

QUESTION: What is the use of such a vast and empty garden?

ANSWER: If you could travel throughout the world and most of the stars with the speed of imagination, you could assert that the world belonged to you. The fact that angels, other people, and animals share this space with you would not negate your assertion. The meaning of the Tradition, "Some people of Paradise will be given a Paradise that would take 500 years to traverse on foot," has been explained in The Twenty-eighth Word and "The Treatise on Sincerity" in The Gleams.

Ninth indication: The result of your belief and love of God is the eternal life of Paradise and vision of Him. People of spiritual discovery and seekers of truth all agree that 1,000 years of a happy life in this world is not worth an hour of life in Paradise, and that 1,000 years of life in Paradise is not worth an hour's vision of the Majestic One in His absolute sacred Beauty and defect-free Perfection. Seeing Him is established by the Qur'an and authentic Prophetic Traditions, one of which says: "That vision far excels all the other pleasures of Paradise, so much so that it causes them to be forgotten. After the vision of God, the people of Paradise will have increased in beauty and loveliness to such a degree that the couples will be able to recognize each other only with great difficulty."

All people feel in the depths of their being a great longing to see such great people of the past as Prophet Solomon, famous for his magnificent perfection, and Prophet Joseph, distinguished for his beauty. So compare how deeply desired and yearned for, and with what degree of passion, is our desire to see Him. And remember that one manifestation of His Beauty and Perfection contains all the beauty and perfection of Paradise, which are far more elevated than all the beauty and perfection seen in this world.

> O God, provide us in this world with love of You and of what will draw us near to You, with the uprightness You command, and in the Hereafter with Your Mercy and the vision of You.
>
> Glory be to You! We have no knowledge save what You have taught us. You are All-Knowing, All-Wise. O God, bestow blessings and peace upon him whom You raised as a mercy for all worlds, and upon his Family and Companions. Amen.

NOTE: Do not regard as too lengthy the detailed explanation in this Word's last section. It is short in proportion to its importance and, in fact, requires further elaboration. Truth speaks in The Words in the name of indications from the Qur'an. Truth speaks the truth. If you see anything incorrect, know that it originated from my mind.

Supplication

O Lord! A person knocks on the door of a palace which is not opened to him or her, with the call of him or her who is esteemed in that palace and whose call is familiar with its inhabitants. So, since I am too wretched to knock on the door of the Court of Your Mercy, I knock on it with the call and supplication of Uways al-Qarani, one of Your servants whom You love. Open that Court of Yours to me, as you opened it to him. I call as he did:

> O God, You are my Lord; I am a slave.
> You are the Creator; I am the one created.
> You are the Provider; I am the one provided.
> You are the Owner; I am the one owned.
> You are the Mighty and Glorious;
> I am the one abased and wretched.
> Your are the Absolutely Rich One;
> I am the one absolutely poor.

You are the All-Living; I am the one dead,
You are the All-Permanent; I am the one mortal.
You are the All-Munificent; I am the one miserly.
You are the All-Benevolent; I am the one doing ill.
You are the All-Forgiving; I am the one sinful.
You are the Grand One; I am the one despicable.
You are the All-Strong; I am the one weak.
You are the Giver; I am the one begging.
You are the One Giving Security;
I am the one in fear.
You are the All-Generous;
I am the one in utmost need.
You are the One Answering pleas
I am the one pleading.
You are the All-Healing One;
I am the one sick.

So forgive my sins, spare me, and heal my ills, O God! O All-Sufficing One! O Lord! O Faithful One! O Most Compassionate One! O Healer! O Munificent One! O Restorer to Health! Pardon all my sins, restore me to health from all illnesses, and be pleased with me for all eternity! Through Your Mercy, O Most Merciful of the Merciful!

The end of their call will be: All praise be to God, the Lord of the Worlds.

The Thirty-third Word

Creation Indicates God's Existence and Unity

In the Name of God,
the Merciful, the Compassionate.

> We shall show them Our signs in the outer world and in themselves, until it becomes clear to them that it is the truth. Is it not enough that your Lord is a witness over all things? (41:53)

QUESTION: We would like a brief, concise explanation of how humanity (the microcosm) and the universe (the macrocosm) point to God's necessary Existence and Unity, as well as His Lordship's essential Qualities and Attributes, which the two parts of the comprehensive verse above denote.

ANSWER: The 32 Words written so far are 32 drops from the ocean of the truths poured out by that verse. Your question is answered therein. The following only points to the droplets of a drop from that ocean.

If a miracle-displaying person wants to build a large palace, first he lays the foundation firmly according to his purpose for building it. Next, he skillfully divides it into apartments and rooms and then furnishes and decorates them. After that, he illuminates the palace with electric lights. He shows his other skills and ever-renewed bountifulness by making additions, changes, and transformations in every wing and apartment. He establishes a communication system linking every apartment and room, and opens windows in every room so that his rank and true identity may be shown and the palace's inhabitants may contact him.

Similarly the Creator, Who is beyond compare and called by 1,001 holy Names, such as Wise Ruler and Just Judge, willed to make that palace of the universe, that Tree of Creation, which is the macrocosm. He laid the palace's (and tree's) foundations in 6 "days" and built the main body with the principles of His Wisdom and rules of His eternal Knowledge. Dividing it into levels and branches, He ramified and elaborated it with the principles of His Decree and Destiny. Then He formed and organized creatures in groups, families, and species and ordered the life of each with the principles of His art and favoring.

After that, He adorned each thing and world in a unique way. He adorned the sky with stars and Earth with flowers. He showed His Names in those vast arenas where His universal laws and all-inclusive principles are in force and illuminated them. Following that, by manifesting His Names the Most Merciful and Most Compassionate, He came to the aid of each individual creature, which cried at the pressure of those universal laws.

That means that He has, within His universal and all-inclusive rules, special favors and help, as well as particular manifestations, that encourage every being to turn to Him at any time and ask Him to meet any of its needs. Also, in order to make His Existence and Unity evident, He opened windows on Himself from all apartments, all levels of creation and worlds, all groups of existence and individuals, and all things. Furthermore, He left a phone in every heart.

Now referring those innumerable windows to the all-comprehensive Divine Knowledge, the discussion of which is beyond our capacity, in a happy correspondence with the 33 repetitions of the phrases of glorifying and praising God, and of affirming His Greatness after each prescribed prayer, and under the title of the 33rd Word, we shall be content with a brief allusion to 33 of them originating from the Qur'an's verses.

Thirty-three windows

FIRST WINDOW: All things, particularly living ones, have many needs and demands that are met on time from somewhere unknown and unexpected. Unable to reach their objects by themselves, they cannot meet even the least of their needs. For example, you cannot satisfy even one need of your own outer and external senses and organs. Extend this comparison to all other living beings. These needs and demands, as well as their gratification, point singly and as a whole to an Absolutely Necessary Being's Existence behind the veil of the Unseen and His Oneness. They show Him to the mind with His Names the All-Munificent, Most Compassionate, Trainer and Upbringer, and Provider and Organizer. Can you explain this universal reality displaying wisdom, awareness, and compassion by attributing it to deaf nature, blind force, random coincidence, or lifeless and powerless causes?

SECOND WINDOW: While in the process of formation, things and beings have an infinite variety of potential forms. Each is given, all at once and wisely and with perfect wisdom, a particular, distinct and extremely well-ordered countenance equipped with outer and inner senses. This countenance bears a unique mark that distinguishes the individual from all other members of its species. Thus one's countenance is a very brilliant stamp of Divine Oneness displayed especially by His purposeful choice and preference.

Just as each face bears witness in infinite ways to an All-Wise Maker's Existence and points to His Unique-ness, that stamp of Oneness displayed by all faces shows to the mind's eye that it is a seal belonging to the Creator of all things. To what workshop can you attribute those stamps that cannot be imitated, not to mention the brilliant seal of God's being the Eternally Besought-of-All that they form as a whole?

THIRD WINDOW: The huge army of countless plant and animal species is characterized by perfect measure and order, a complete lack of confusion and forgetfulness, a particular form and garment, and a particular provision and weaponry. In addition, each species is trained and demobilized in a unique way.[37] This is a stamp of the One of Unity, a stamp as brilliant as the sun and thus beyond doubt.

Who but the One with limitless Power, all-encompassing Knowledge, and infinite Wisdom can dare to share in that infinitely wonderful administration? If one who could not administer and train all species and races together, even though they are intermixed, were to interfere with one of them, confusion would arise. However, we read: *Turn your gaze again, do you see any fissure?* (67:3). As there is no sign of any void or confusion, no one could have a part in creation.

FOURTH WINDOW: Seeds pray in the tongue of their disposition and potentiality, animals pray in the tongue of their natural needs, and all who are compelled to do so pray in the tongue of compulsion. Each prayer is answered. As each answered prayer bears witness to and points to God's nec-

---

[37] Among those species are some whose numbers in a year exceed all people who have ever lived, and who ever will live, from the time of Adam to the end of the world.

essary Existence and Unity, all of them point to an All-Compassionate, All-Munificent, and All-Answering Creator as a whole and on a larger scale.

FIFTH WINDOW: We see that things, especially living ones, apparently come into existence as if all at once. Given this, we would expect them to be simple, coarse, and without any art. Instead, they are so finely created that many skills are required, embellished so carefully and delicately that a long time is demanded, ornamented so artistically that many tools are needed, and made so elaborately that a great amount of material is necessary. So the beautiful form given to each and all things simultaneously, as well as the wonderful artistry manifested on them, testify to an All-Wise Maker's necessary Existence and point to His Lordship's Unity. As a whole and through their form, as well as their displayed artistry, they point in a most brilliant way to a Necessarily Existent Being Who is infinitely powerful and wise.

How do you explain this? Can it be attributed to ignorant nature? Can you call that Holy Maker "nature" and ascribe the miracles of His Power to it? This is the greatest mistake, and regarding it as so is inconceivable.

SIXTH WINDOW: Consider the following verse:

> In the creation of the heavens and Earth; in the alternation of night and day; in the sailing of the ships through the ocean for the benefit of humanity; in the water which God sends down from the sky and with which He revives Earth after its death, and dispersing over it all kinds of beasts; in the ordinance of the winds and clouds that are driven between Earth and sky, are signs for people who have sense and use their reason. (2:164)

This verse, which shows God's necessary Existence and Unity, is an extremely large window through which one of God's Greatest Names is seen. Briefly, all worlds situated at the universe's various levels point to the same result in different tongues: the Lordship of a single Wise Maker. Just as well-organized and systematic movements in the heavens end in great results and thereby show a Majestic All-Powerful One's Existence and Unity and His Lordship's perfection, the tremendous seasonal and other changes we see on Earth result in great, comprehensive benefits and thereby show the necessity of that

Majestic All-Powerful One's Unity and His Lordship's perfection.

All land and water animals are fed through perfect mercy, given forms with perfect wisdom, and equipped with senses and faculties through perfect Lordship. Each testifies to that Majestic All-Powerful One's Existence and points to His Unity. As a whole, they display His Divinity's grandeur and His Lordship's perfection on a large scale. Similarly, all well-formed plants in gardens and orchards and their ornate flowers, the well-proportioned fruits that replace the flowers, and the rich embellishments displayed by the fruits bear witness to that All-Wise Maker's Existence and point to His Unity individually. Collectively, they show His Mercy's grace and His Lordship's perfection in a splendid way.

All drops sent from the atmosphere and charged with important purposes, necessary consequences, and benefits show that All-Wise Maker's necessary Existence and Unity and His Lordship's perfection. In the same way, all mountains and minerals deposited in them for various purposes show that Wise Maker's Existence and Unity and His Lordship's perfection.

All beautiful flowers decorating hills and plains individually attest to an All-Wise Maker's necessary Existence and point to His Unity. Collectively, they show His Sovereignty's majesty and His Lordship's perfection. All well-proportioned shapes and positions of herb and tree leaves, as well as their rapturous and systematic movements, show that All-Wise Maker's necessary Existence and Unity and His Lordship's perfection.

All growing bodies have been innately equipped with various members and systems to grow. At the time of growth, they begin to move in an ordered manner and are directed toward yielding fruits. Each one testifies to that All-Wise Maker's necessary Existence and points to His Unity.

As a whole, they demonstrate His Power's comprehensiveness, His Wisdom's inclusiveness, His art's beauty, and His Lordship's perfection on a very large scale. Establishing souls and spirits in all animal bodies with perfect wisdom, equipping them with appropriate systems with perfect order, and mobilizing them for unique services and purposes with perfect wisdom—all of this bears witness and points to that All-Wise Maker's necessary Existence and Unity. Collectively, these acts show His Mercy and His Lordship's perfection in a most brilliant way.

All Divine inspirations that instruct humanity in knowledge and truth, as well as teach animals how to procure their needs, suggest the Existence of a Most Compassionate Lord and point to His Lordship. Also, like rays of light coming from the eye and collecting together all visible objects each of which is a "flower" in the garden of the universe, each outer and inner sense functions as a key to a different world. This demonstrates, as brightly as the sun, the necessary Existence of that All-Wise Maker, All-Knowing Originator, Most Compassionate Creator, All-Munificent Provider, and His Unity and Lordship's perfection.

Thus the huge window consisting of 12 openings in 12 places shows 12 colors of Almighty God's Oneness and Uniqueness and His Lordship's perfection through a light of truth. How can you close that window, which is as wide as Earth or even its orbit? How can you extinguish that source of light, which is as bright as the sun? Behind what veil of heedlessness can you hide it?

SEVENTH WINDOW: Infinite kinds and species of creatures come into existence easily and resemble each other in many ways. They are spread on Earth with perfect order and show a perfect proportionateness and equipment. This demonstrates an All-Wise Maker's necessary Existence and Unity and His Power's perfection on a broad scale. The creation of innumerable and unique well-composed compound beings out of simple lifeless elements also testifies to that All-Wise Maker's necessary Existence and points to His Unity. As a whole, these beings show His Power's perfection and His Unity in a most brilliant way.

Also, there is an infinite degree of differentiation and compounding within infinite profusion. For example, while seeds and roots exist underground in very confused positions, they are amazingly distinguished in growth. Like food particles entering the body in confusion and then separated and shared among organs and tissues with perfect measure and wisdom, atoms entering trees in confusion are distinguished and distributed among leaves, blossoms, and fruits.

This shows the necessary Existence of that absolutely Wise, Knowing, and Powerful One, as well as His Unity and His Power's perfection. It also displays His Lordship's grandeur and perfection, for He makes the world of atoms into a boundless, vast field and then sows and harvests it every moment with perfect wisdom. He obtains fresh crops of different worlds from it and causes those unconscious, powerless, and ignorant atoms to perform innumerable systematic functions, just as if they were extremely learned, conscious, and capable.

Thus a large window is opened onto knowledge of God through these four ways that display the All-Wise Maker to the mind on a large scale. If you do not want to see Him in this way and recognize Him, rid yourself of reason so as to become like an animal and be saved (if such a thing is even possible)!

EIGHTH WINDOW: The testimony of all Prophets (those people with luminous spirits), based on their manifest and evident miracles; the testimony of all saints (those distinguished with illumined hearts), relying on their wonder-making and spiritual discoveries; and the testimony of all purified scholars (those with enlightened minds who rely on their research and quest for truth), all testify to the necessary Existence and Unity of One, the Creator of all things, and His Power's perfection.

They form a vast and enlightening window through which His Lordship—sustaining, training, raising, etc.—shows itself continually. Who do you rely on so that you do not heed those people? Or, by closing your eyes in the daytime, do you imagine the world to be in darkness?

NINTH WINDOW: All beings' worship shows an Absolutely Worshipped One. Those who penetrate the World of Spirits and the inner dimension of things, where they meet with angels and spirit beings, testify that all angels and spirit beings worship an Eternally Worshipped One in perfect obedience. We all observe that all living beings perform duties in perfect order in a manner resembling worship, and that all inanimate things render services with perfect submission in a like manner. All of this shows a True Object of Worship's necessary Existence and Unity.

This is also the case with the true knowledge of all saints knowing Him (which bears the weight of consensus), all thankful people's fruitful thanks, the blessed recitations of those who recite God's Names, the praises (which increase Divine bounties) of those who praise God, the pronouncements and descriptions of Divine Unity (based on decisive proofs) of those who believe in it, the true love of all lovers of God, the true will and desires of those who seek Him, and the earnest searching and inclinations of those who turn to Him. All of this shows the necessary Existence and Unity of that Eternally Worshipped One, the One Who is Recognized, Mentioned, Praised, Beloved, Desired, and Sought, as well as His Lordship's perfection.

Also, the acceptable worship and supplications of perfected people, as well as their spiritual radiance, visions, and illuminations, demonstrate that Everlasting and Eternally Worshipped One's necessary Existence and Unity and His Lordship's perfection. These three aspects open up a broad, light-giving window onto Divine Unity.

TENTH WINDOW: Consider these verses:

> And He sends down water from the heaven and brings forth with it crops and fruits as provision for you, and He has made subject to you the ships so that they sail through the sea by His command, and He has made the rivers sub-

> ject to you; and He has made subject to you the sun and the moon, both pursuing their courses, and He has made subject to you the night and the day; and He gives you of all that you ask Him. If you were to count God's bounties, you could not enumerate them. (14:32-34)

The mutual helping and solidarity of beings and their responding to each other's call for assistance shows that all creatures are trained by one Instructor, administered by one Director, controlled by one Disposer, and serve one Master. Through a universal law of mutual helping, the sun cooks, by the Lord's command, that which is needed by Earth's living creatures to continue living. The moon acts as a calendar; light, air, water, and sustenance hasten to help animate beings; plants hasten to help animals; animals and plants hasten to help human beings; bodily members hasten to help each other; and food particles hasten to help cells.

This most wise and generous cooperation among unconscious beings, their responding to each other's needs and supporting each other under a law of munificence and grace, a law of compassion and care and a principle of mercy, show that they are the servants, officers, and creatures of a unique One of Unity, a peerless, Eternally-Besought-of-All, an Absolutely Powerful, Absolutely Knowledgeable, Absolutely Compassionate, Absolutely Munificent, and Necessarily-Existent One. How do you, O follower of materialistic philosophy and scientism, respond to this mighty window? Can chance have a hand in this?

ELEVENTH WINDOW: Consider the following verse:

> Beware, only in the remembrance of God do hearts find rest. (13:28)

Only through recognizing their One Creator can all spirits and hearts be delivered from the distress and confusion of misguidance, and from the spiritual pains arising from that distress. Attributing all beings to a Maker of Unity allows them to find rest in the remembrance of One God. As proved in The Twenty-second Word, if a single being did not create the innumerable creatures of creation, one thing must be ascribed to numberless causes.

If this is the case, it becomes practically impossible to explain the existence of a single thing.

Consider this: If one soldier is commanded by 100 officers, 100 difficulties will arise. But if 100 soldiers are commanded by one officer, they will be as easy to command as one soldier. This also is true in the case of creation, for creating one thing by multiple causes would face as many problems as there are causes. Given this, belief in the Creator's Unity and God's Knowledge will deliver us from the endless distress arising from the curiosity and desire to find the truth inherent in our nature.

Unbelief and associating partners with God engenders so many difficulties and pains that they clearly cannot contain any truth. In contrast, we see how easily things and beings come into existence in great variety and multiplicity and yet with utmost beauty and artistry.

This ease of creation can be explained only by ascribing all of creation to One God. As there is infinite ease in the way of believing in One God, it is certainly necessary and the truth itself. See how dark and distressing is the way of misguidance. Why do you take it, when you can see how easy and pleasant is the way of belief and affirming Divine Unity? Take that way and be delivered.

TWELFTH WINDOW: As declared in:

> Glorify the Name of your Lord, the Most High, Who has created and made well-proportioned and orderly; and Who has determined (the shape, lifespan, and nature of all things) and guided (each one toward its own way) (87:1-3),

all things, especially living ones, have a form and well-measured proportions according to their functions, as if they have emerged from a mold of wisdom. Each has been given a unique shape, with curves and twists according to its expected benefits and uses. Their resulting outer and inner changes and renewals proceed according to certain determined measures and purposes.

All of this shows that the shapes and proportions of these innumerable creatures are planned within the frame of an all-inclusive Determining by an All-Powerful One of Majesty, an All-Wise One of Perfection. Their being given forms and bodies in the workshop of Divine Power points to His necessary Existence and bears witness in endless tongues to His Unity and His Power's perfection.

Look at your own body and its parts. Reflect on the uses and benefits of each one's curves and twists, and see the perfection of the Power embedded in perfect Wisdom!

THIRTEENTH WINDOW: As stated in: *There is nothing that does not glorify Him with praise* (17:44), each thing mentions and glorifies its Creator in its own tongue. These glorifications, whether vocal or in the tongue of their lives and dispositions, show a single Holy One's Existence.

The testimony of disposition or nature is not rejected. The proof produced by practical life, especially when it issues from many aspects of that life, cannot provoke doubt. See how each well-ordered form of these creatures, which testify through their innate dispositions and bear witness in the language of their lives and manners, and which all turn to a single center like concentric circles, is an expressive tongue. Their well-proportioned structures and organizations are tongues of testimony, and their well-organized lives are tongues of glorification.

As argued in The Twenty-fourth Word, these glorifications and exaltations testify to a single Most Holy Being, display His necessary Existence as certainly as light shows the sun, and point to His Divinity's perfection.

FOURTEENTH WINDOW: Consider the following verses:

> Say: "In whose hand is the dominion of all things?" (23:88)
>
> There is nothing but its treasuries are with us. (15:21)
>
> There is not a moving creature but He grasps its forelock. (11:56)
>
> Surely my Lord records and preserves all things. (11:57)

These verses state that everything, in all circumstances and aspects of its life and existence, needs a single Creator of Majesty. Looking at creatures, we see an absolute force within absolute weakness and impressions and inscriptions of an absolute power in absolute impotence. For example, awakening the life-force in plant seeds and roots is extraordinary.

There also are manifestations of absolute wealth within absolute poverty and sterility, like the poverty of Earth and trees in winter and their glittering profusion in spring. Sparks of absolute life are observed in absolutely lifeless matter (e.g., the transformation of mineral elements into living entities). Displays of all-encompassing consciousness are seen in absolute ignorance, as when everything acts as if consciously conforming to the universe's order, life's principles, and wisdom's demands. Such manifestations open windows onto the necessary Existence and Unity of One Absolutely Powerful, Strong, Rich, and Knowing, as well as Living and Self-Subsistent. In their totality, they point to a luminous highway (the way of believing in God and His Oneness) on a large scale.

If you ascribe creativity to nature and accept it as self-originated instead of recognizing Divine Power, you must acknowledge that everything contains an infinite force and power, wisdom and skill, and the capacity to see, know, and direct most other things.

FIFTEENTH WINDOW: As declared in: *He has created everything in the best way* (32:7), everything is clothed with perfect measure and order in a form tailored to its nature's receptivity. Everything is assembled with the finest art, by the most direct method, in the best shape and the easiest manner, and in the most practicable structure. Look at the "dress" of birds and see how easily they can ruffle or set their feathers and yet use them continually. Giving things bodies and dressing them in forms in a wise manner without waste and futility bears witness, to the number of those things, to an All-Wise Maker's necessary Existence and points to an Absolutely Powerful and Knowing One.

SIXTEENTH WINDOW: The order and organization in creation and the management of creatures, recruited every season on Earth, show a universal purposiveness and wisdom. Since an attribute cannot be without the one it qualifies, that universal wisdom shows a Wise One. The wonderful adornment within that veil of wisdom shows an all-embracing grace, which shows a Gracious, Munificent Creator.

The all-encompassing favoring and benevolence within that veil of grace show an all-encompassing mercy, which shows an All-Merciful, All-Compassionate One. The sustenance and provision of all living creatures on that veil of mercy, all perfect and appropriate for their needs, show an upbringing and training providence and a compassionate Lordship. That training and administering show an All-Munificent Provider.

Each creature, having been raised with perfect wisdom, adorned with perfect graciousness, favored with perfect mercy, and nurtured with perfect caring and compassion, bears witness to the necessary Existence of an All-Wise, Munificent, Compassionate, Providing Maker and points to His Unity.

Consider the all-encompassing wisdom manifested on Earth, which clearly shows a purpose and will. Consider the perfect grace encompassing all creatures in accordance with wisdom; the all-embracing mercy comprising both grace and wisdom and touching all creatures; and the most generous sustaining and nurturing comprising the mercy, wisdom, and grace touching all living creatures.

Just as the seven colors form the light and the light illuminating Earth shows the sun, that grace within wisdom, mercy within grace, and sustaining and nurturing within mercy show brilliantly, and on a vast scale and at a high degree, the Unity and Lordship of a Most Wise, Munificent, Compassionate, Providing, and Necessarily-Existent One.

How can you explain this wise as well as compassionate, generous, providential sustaining and raising; this extraordinary, wonderful, miraculous state of affairs before your eyes? By random chance and coincidence, blind force, deaf and mute nature, or by powerless, lifeless, and ignorant causes? By giving the name of "nature," which is infinitely impotent, ignorant, deaf, blind, contingent, and helpless, to the All-Majestic One, Who is infinitely Powerful, Knowing, Hearing, and Seeing? Do you want to commit such a serious mistake? How can you extinguish a truth as brilliant as the sun? Under what veil of heedlessness can you hide it?

SEVENTEENTH WINDOW: Consider the following verse:

> Surely in the heavens and Earth are signs for believers. (45:3)

Consider the following points:

- During summer we see an infinite generosity and absolute liberality, which could be expected to cause disorder and confusion, within an infinite order and harmony. See all the plants adorning Earth's face.

- The absolute speed in creating things, which normally would result in imbalance and loss of decorum, is observed within a perfect equilibrium. See all the fruits adorning Earth's face.

Creation Indicates God's Existence and Unity

- The absolute multiplicity and variety, which normally would bring about triviality and even ugliness, is apparent within art's perfect beauty. See all the flowers gilding Earth's face.

- The absolute ease in creating things, which normally would cause simplicity and lack of art, is seen within an art, skill, and attention of infinite degree. See all the seeds, which are like tiny containers and programs of all plants and trees, and also like small cases containing their life-histories.

- The great distances, which normally would necessitate difference and diversity, appear within an absolute correspondence and conformity. See all the varieties of cereal grains sown throughout the world.

- The utter intermingling, which normally would cause confusion and mess, is seen within perfect differentiation and separation. Consider how seeds, cast into the ground all mixed together and resembling each other with regard to their substance, are perfectly differentiated when they are about to sprout. See how the various substances entering trees are separated perfectly for leaves, blossoms, and fruits, and how the foods entering the stomach all mixed together are separated perfectly for the body's members and cells. Consider all this and see the perfect power within perfect wisdom.

- The infinite abundance and profusion, which normally would cause triviality and worthlessness, are seen to be most valuable and most worthwhile in regard to Earth's creatures and art. Among all those infinite wonders of art, consider only the varieties of mulberry, those sweets of Divine Power, on the table of the All-Merciful One on Earth, and observe the perfect mercy combined with the perfect art.

Just as daytime shows light and light shows the sun, the great value despite infinite profusion; within infinite profusion, the infinite differentiation and separation despite boundless intermingling; within infinite differentiation and separation, the infinite conformity and resemblance despite great distances; within infinite resemblance, the infinite care and attention in the making despite infinite ease and facility; within the most beautiful making, the infinite equilibrium, balance, and lack of waste despite absolute speed and rapidity; within the utmost lack of waste, the highest degree of beauty of art despite the utmost abundance and multiplicity; within the highest degree of art, the absolute order and harmony despite the utmost liberality—all of these bear witness to the necessary Existence, Unity, and Oneness of an All-Powerful One of Majesty, an All-Wise One of Perfection, an All-Compassionate One of Grace and Beauty, and His Power's perfection and His Lordship's grace and beauty. They demonstrate the meaning of: *His are the Most Beautiful Names* (20:8).

So, unfortunate, obstinate, and heedless one! How can you interpret this mighty truth or explain this infinitely miraculous and wonderful state of affairs? To what can you attribute these truly extraordinary arts? What veil of heedlessness can you draw across this window as broad as Earth and then close it?

Where is your chance and coincidence? Where is your unconscious companion on which you rely and call "nature," your friend and support in misguidance? Is it not impossible for chance and coincidence to have a hand in these affairs? To attribute to nature even a minute fraction of ordering these things is completely impossible. Or does lifeless, ignorant, unconscious nature have machines and printing presses within each thing, made from each, and equal in quantity to the number of individual things?

EIGHTEENTH WINDOW: Consider the following verse:

> Have they not considered the truth contained in the inner dimension of the heavens and Earth? (7:185)

and the comparison explained in The Twenty-second Word:

A perfect, well-designed and artistic construction like a palace points to a perfect act—that is, a building points to an act of construction. A perfect, well-performed act points to a perfect actor, to a skillful master-builder. The title of a skillful master-builder points to a perfect attribute, to an artistic ability. A perfect attribute, a perfect competence in an art points to the existence of a perfect capacity. A prefect capacity or potentiality points to the existence of a noble spirit, an exalted being.

Likewise, the ever-renewed, refreshed, and replaced works filling Earth's face and the universe show acts of perfect degree. Those acts, occurring in an infinitely wise and well-ordered system, show an agent or an actor with perfect titles and names. Just as well-arranged and wise acts must have someone doing them, infinitely perfect titles point to that agent's infinitely perfect attributes.

According to grammar, active participles and nouns denoting one who does something are derived from verbs. In Arabic, nouns originate in adjectives. Perfect attributes point to perfect personal potentialities, and perfect potentialities point to the one with a limitless degree of perfection.

Thus, since each work of art and all creatures in the universe are perfect, and since each bears witness to an act, the act to a name, the name to an attribute, the attribute to a potentiality, and the potentiality to a being, then—as well as all of them testifying to a single Maker of Majesty's necessary Existence and Unity—as a whole they constitute a stairway of knowledge of God, which leads to Him in a form as strong as the chain of creatures, and a proof of truth in series that cannot be doubted.

So, O poor, heedless unbeliever, can you break

this proof as strong as the chain of beings? Can you shut up this window that has innumerable openings to show the rays of truth? What veil of heedlessness can you draw across it?

NINETEENTH WINDOW: Consider the following verse:

> The seven heavens and Earth and all in them glorify Him. There is nothing that does not glorify Him. (17:44)

According to the meaning of this verse, the Majestic Maker has attached so many instances of wisdom and meanings to heavenly bodies that, as if to express His Majesty and Grace, He has adorned the heavens with suns, moons, and stars. He has attached such instances of wisdom and meanings to the creatures in the atmosphere as if to make the atmosphere speak in words like lightning, thunder, and raindrops. He also teaches His perfect Wisdom and His Mercy's beauty.

Just as He makes Earth speak in meaningful words like plants and animals, and thereby shows His art's perfection to the universe, He shows His art's perfection and His Mercy's beauty by making plants and trees speak in their words of leaves, flowers, and fruits. By making flowers and fruits speak in words of seeds and pollen, He teaches the subtleties of His art and His Lordship's perfection to conscious beings. Among these countless words of glorification, we shall consider the manner in which a flower or an ear of wheat expresses its glorification and discover how it bears witness.

Each plant and tree shows its Maker in numerous tongues in a way that amazes observers and causes them to say: "All glory be to God, how excellently it bears witness." Each plant's glorifications when it blossoms and grows ears or spikes—the time when it speaks in smiles—are beautiful like itself and evident. The order or system showing the wisdom or purposiveness expressed in all flowers' speaking, in the tongues of well-formed spikes or ears, and in the words of well-proportioned seeds and well-made grains, points (in a measure) to knowledge.

The measure is in the art's skillful design, which, in turn, is in an adornment showing grace and munificence. The adornment is in agreeable fragrances showing mercy and benevolence. These meaningful states of things, one within the other, form such a tongue of testimony that they define their Majestic Maker with His Names, describe Him with His Attributes, exemplify His Names' manifestations, and express His being loved and recognized.

Hearing such a testimony from a flower, if you can hear the voices of all flowers in all of the Lord's gardens on Earth's face and how powerfully they announce the Majestic Maker's necessary Existence and Unity, how can you still have any questions, doubts, and hesitations?

Look at a tree that blossoms in spring. Its leaves are regular, its blossoms proportionate, its fruits grow and ripen in wisdom and mercy, and the tree dances with breezes. Consider its fine expressiveness and exact balance in the wise order shown by the words of fruits smiling with a display of mercy, the tongue of blossoms smiling with a joy of grace, leaves becoming green with a hand of munificence. Consider the delicate arts and designs in the balance showing justice and exact measure, the sweet smells showing mercy and benevolence in skillfully made designs and ornaments, and the seeds and stones, each a miracle of Power in sweet tastes.

Such facts show the necessary Existence and

Unity of an All-Wise Maker, All-Munificent, All-Compassionate, All-Benevolent, Bestower of Bounties, All-Beautifying, One Making Excellent, and His Mercy's beauty and His Lordship's perfection. If you could hear all the tongues of all trees' dispositions, you would see what beautiful gems there are in the treasury of: *Whatever is in the heavens and Earth glorifies God* (61:1).

So, O unfortunate heedless one who supposes yourself to be free to feel ingratitude! If you do not want to recognize an All-Munificent One of Majesty, Who makes Himself known to you and wills to be loved by you in such innumerable tongues, then these tongues should be silenced. But since they cannot be silenced, you should listen to them. Just closing your ears will not make you indifferent to them or able to escape from them, for the universe does not stop speaking and creatures are not silenced. As testifiers to Divine Unity cannot be silenced, they will condemn you.

TWENTIETH WINDOW[38]: Consider the following verses:

> Glory be to Him in Whose hand is the

---

[38] The truth in this Twentieth Window occurred to me in Arabic as given below:

dominion of all things. (36:83)

There is nothing but its treasuries are with Us and We send it not down but with a known, determined measure. We loose the winds as fertilizing drivers of

---

The radiance of light is through Your illuminating
and making things known through it;
The succession of ages like waves is through
Your dispatching and employing them.
Glory be to You, how mighty is Your rule!
The gushing out and flowing forth of rivers is through
Your storing them up and subjugating them.
The formation and decoration of stones is through
Your arranging and fashioning them.
Glory be to You, how unique
and splendid is Your Wisdom!
The smiling of flowers is through
Your adorning and beautifying them.
The emergence of fruits in splendor is through
Your bestowal and favoring.
Glory be to You, how beautiful is Your Art!
The singing of birds is through Your making them
speak and communicate with each other.
The hymning of rain is through
Your sending it down, Your bestowal.
Glory be to You, how vast is Your Mercy!
The motion of moons is through Your determining,
arranging, directing, and illuminating.
Glory be to You, how brilliant Your proofs,
how clear Your evidences!

> clouds to make an (electric) current between them and send down from the sky blessed water and provide you with it; you are not the ones who store it. (15:21-22)

A work of art's perfect wisdom, grace, and beauty are apparent in particulars, results, and details. Similarly all universal elements, which seem to be in confusion as well as random and coincidental, assume positions dictated by wisdom and art. Thus light radiates to show and expose God's creatures. In other words, an All-Wise Maker uses light to make His unique arts visible in this world.

Consider the following: Wind, as seen by its other great and wise benefits and functions, runs to carry out its vital duties. Thus, its wave-like movements show that it is employed, sent, and used by an All-Wise Maker. Such movements display the rapid carrying out of the Lords' orders. Springs, streams, and rivers do not emerge from the ground and mountains by chance. Rather, their benefits and uses (the results of Divine Mercy), their storage in mountains according to need, and their being sent according to wisdom show that an All-Wise Lord has subjugated and stored them and causes them to well up in obedience to His commands.

Stones, jewels, and minerals have specific purposes and benefits and are arranged to meet human and animal needs. This shows that an All-Wise Maker has decorated, arranged, organized, and fashioned their decorativeness and beneficial properties. Each flower and fruit, all of which have many smiles, tastes, beauties, embroideries, and scents, is like an invitation and menu on the table of an All-Munificent Maker, a Compassionate Bestower of Bounties. They are given as various invitations and menus to each species through their specific colors, scents, and tastes.

Birds vocalize in an amazing way to relay their feelings and express their intentions to other birds. This clearly indicates that they twitter and chirp because an All-Wise Maker has enabled them to do so. Clouds are also amazing. The sound of falling raindrops, as well as the noise of thunder and lightning, are not meaningless; rather, these strange atmospheric events occur and, as a result, raindrops fall and feed all living creatures on Earth, which are needy and long for them. Thus these events are meaningful and full of purposive wisdom. At an All-Munificent Lord's command, the rain calls out to those longing for it: "Good news! I am coming!"

Look at just the moon among the sky's innumerable bodies. The important instances of wisdom connecting it with Earth, as discussed elsewhere in the *Risale-i Nur*, demonstrate that it moves at the command of an All-Powerful and Wise One. These universal elements open a vast window. They proclaim and show a Necessarily Existent One's Unity, His Power's perfection, and His Sovereignty's grandeur.

So, O heedless one, if you can silence this voice resounding like the crashing of thunder, as well as extinguish this light as brilliant as the sun, forget God. Otherwise, come to your senses and say: *All glory be to Him Whom the seven heavens and Earth and all within them glorify* (17:44).

TWENTY-FIRST WINDOW: Consider this verse:

> The sun runs its course to its place destined, that is the determining of the All-Mighty, the All-Knowing. (36:38)

The sun, the universe's lamp, is a window onto the Maker of the universe's Existence and Unity, which are as brilliant and radiant as the sun itself. Despite their great differences in size, position, and speed, the 12 planets move and revolve with perfect order, wisdom, balance, and without confusion. Bound to the sun through a Divine law known as gravity, they follow their leader and thereby show on a large scale the Divine Power's grandeur and the Lord's Unity. Just imagine how tremendous a Power and Wisdom are engaged in rotating those lifeless bodies, those vast, unconscious masses, so perfectly, and in using them as He wills.

If any degree of chance were to interfere in this vast and complex event, it would cause such a great explosion that the universe would be ripped apart. If it were to stop a planet's motion for even a minute, that planet would leave its orbit and collide with another planet. Imagine the awesome collision of bodies thousands of times larger than Earth.

Referring the solar system's wonders to God's All-Encompassing Knowledge, we consider only our own Earth. We see it make a long journey around the sun due to the Lord's command to carry out a most important duty and in a way showing the grandeur of the Lord's imperial Power and

Majesty, the loftiness of Divine Sovereignty, and the perfection of His Mercy and Wisdom.[39]

Like a ship ordered by the Lord, it has been filled with God's wonderful creatures and made like a moving place of recreation for His conscious servants. The moon has been attached to it with precise reckoning for mighty instances of wisdom, like being an hour-hand telling the time and given various mansions through which to journey. These aspects of this blessed planet prove an All-Powerful One's necessary Existence and Unity with a testimony as strong as Earth itself. You can make an analogy with the rest of the solar system from this.

Moreover, the sun turns on its axis like a spinning-wheel in order to wind the immaterial threads called gravity into a ball, and then uses them to tie planets and set them in order. One theory says the sun and its planets are driven at a high speed toward the constellation Lyra (the "sun of suns"). This occurs by the All-Majestic One's Power and command, the Monarch of Eternity. It is as if He makes the solar system

---

[39] This is described in The Third Letter. Said Nursi, *The Letters*.

move like an army of soldiers under orders, thereby showing His Lordship's majesty.

So, O astronomer, can chance have a hand in these affairs? Tell me what causes can reach them, what force can draw close to this! Would such an All-Majestic Sovereign display impotence and give others a share in His Sovereignty? Would He give this, especially living beings, which are the universe's fruit, result, aim, and cream, to other hands?

Would He permit others to interfere? Would He leave us to our own devices, even though we are the most comprehensive fruit, the most perfect result, His guest and vicegerent on Earth (one who must rule according to His laws), and serve as a mirror (reflecting His Names)? Would He leave us to nature and chance, thereby reducing His Sovereignty's majesty and His perfect Wisdom to nothing?

TWENTY-SECOND WINDOW: Consider the following verses:

> Have We not made Earth a cradle, and the mountains masts? We have created you as pairs. (78:6-8)
>
> Look at the imprints of God's Mercy, how He revives Earth after its death!

(30:50)

Earth is like a head containing innumerable mouths with innumerable tongues, each of which has innumerable proofs testifying in innumerable ways to an All-Majestic One's necessary Existence and Unity, to One Who is powerful over all things and knows everything, and to His sacred Attributes and Beautiful Names.

At first, Earth was a liquid matter that was transformed into a rock stratum. Earth [as we know it] was made out of this rock. If it had retained its liquid form, it would have been uninhabitable. If it had remained as rock, hard like iron, it would not have been suitable for us. And so we know that an All-Wise Maker's Wisdom, One Who is aware of the needs of Earth's inhabitants, gave it its present form.

Earth's stratum of soil was laid over the feet of mast-like mountains, which provide an outlet for its internal quakes and so it could continue its duty and movements without diversion. Mountains protect Earth's surface from the oceans' invasion. They are treasuries for the vital necessities of living creatures, air filters that purify the air of harmful gasses, store water, and are sources of necessary minerals. Given this, as well as their other duties and aspects, mountains testify to an Absolutely Powerful, All-Wise, Compassionate One's necessary Existence and Unity.

So, O geologist, how do you explain this? Could chance have made this Divine ship a display of wonders, full of wonderful creatures? Can chance cause this ship to travel at an incredible speed without losing anything arranged on its surface? Look at the wonderful kinds of art on Earth's face. See how wisely elements have been charged with duties, how beautifully they look after the All-Merciful One's guests here at the command of a Powerful, Wise One, and hasten to serve them!

Among unique and wonderful works of art, consider those lines of embroidery on Earth's multicolored face that display striking instances of wisdom. See how He makes brooks and streams, seas and rivers, mountains and hills serve as dwellings and transport for some of His creatures and servants. Innumerable tongues testify to an All-Powerful One of Majesty's necessary Existence and Unity, to an All-Wise One of Perfection Who populates Earth with countless plant and animal species in perfect wisdom and order; Who causes it to prosper with life; Who discharges those inhabitants in regular cycles from their duties through death; and Who regularly refills it and revives it after its death in a way analogous to the Resurrection.

In short, Earth's face exhibits the wonders of His art, is an assembly arena of exquisite creatures, a thoroughfare for the troops of creatures, and a place of worship and dwelling for His servants. It is like the universe's heart, and so shows a light of Divine Unity as broad as the universe.

So, O geographer! If you do not recognize God while Earth's head makes Him known via innumerable mouths containing infinite tongues, and if you submerge your head in the swamp of naturalism, consider the extent of your error. Becoming aware of the severe punishment you will thereby deserve, come to your senses. Raise your head from the swamp and say: "I believe in God, in Whose hands is the dominion of all things!"

TWENTY-THIRD WINDOW: Consider the following verse:

> He created death and life. (67:2)

Life is Divine Power's most luminous and

beautiful miracle, Divine Unity's most brilliant and strongest proof, the most comprehensive and polished mirror reflecting the Eternally-Besought-of-All. Life manifests the Ever-Living and Self-Subsistent One with all His Names and essential Qualities, for it is a compounded light formed by the manifestations of many Divine Attributes together, just as the seven colors are compounded in light and various medicinal substances in natural confections.

Similarly, life is a reality compounded of many Divine Attributes' manifestations causing it to have many attributes. Some of these attributes develop through senses and become distinct. Most of them, however, make themselves felt through sentiments, feelings and emotions and known as a result of life's "boiling."

Life also comprises providence, mercy, grace, and wisdom, which are the most substantial elements in maintaining and administering the universe. It is as if life brings them along wherever it goes. For example, when life enters a body, the Name the All-Wise also shows itself therein and builds and arranges that "nest" of life with perfect wisdom. The Names the All-Munificent and All-

Compassionate manifest at the same instant, furnish and decorate that nest in accordance with its needs, and, respectively, bestow on it all kinds of favors to continue and perfect that life. And, the Name the Provider shows Itself by supplying life with the material and spiritual nourishment necessary for its maintenance and flourishing, as well as by storing a certain amount of that nourishment in its body.

This means that life is like a focal point at which various Names or Attributes meet or, rather, are united into each other to form one entity. It is as if life is entirely knowledge while simultaneously being power, wisdom, mercy, and so on. Due to its comprehensive nature, life is a mirror to the Eternally-Besought-of-All that reflects the essential Qualities of the Divine Being's Essence. As a result, the Necessarily Existent One, the Ever-Living and Self-Subsistent, creates and shows life in the greatest profusion. He also concentrates all things around life to make them serve it, for life is entrusted with a very important duty.

It is not easy to be a mirror to God as the Eternally-Besought-of-All. The innumerable new lives and spirits, as well as the essences or identities of lives, that we constantly witness being brought into existence instantly and from nothing show the necessary Existence, sacred Attributes, and Beautiful Names of the Necessarily Existent, Ever-Living and Self-Subsistent One, just as rays of light show the sun. If you do not recognize the sun and admit its existence, you have to deny the light pervading daytime.

In the same way, if you deny the Sun of Oneness, the Ever-Living and Self-Subsistent, the Giver of Life and the One Causing to Die, you have to deny the existence of all living beings on this planet from their appearance to Earth's final destruction. You would have to admit to yourself that you are like the unconscious, most ignorant beings.

TWENTY-FOURTH WINDOW: Consider the following verse:

> There is no god but He. All things are perishing except His "Face;" His is the sovereignty and unto Him you are being returned. (28:88)

Death is a proof of Divine Lordship to the degree of life, a very strong evidence of His Oneness. According to the meaning of: *He has created death and life* (67:2), death is neither total non-existence or extinction, nor absolute annihilation or decay without one who authors it. Rather, as the First Letter points out,[40] it is a discharge from worldly service by an All-Wise Author, a change of place and bodily renewal, a freeing from duties, a release from the body's prison, a predetermined and well-ordered work of wisdom.

Just as Earth's lively face, as well as its creatures and animate beings, testify to an All-Wise Maker's necessary Existence and Unity, so do those living creatures bear witness through their death to an Ever-Living, Permanent One's Oneness and Eternity. As such matters were explained in The Twenty-second Word, we will explain here only the following subtle point.

Through their lives, all living beings testify to a Necessarily Existent One's Existence; through their death, they all bear witness to an Ever-Living Permanent One's Eternity and Oneness. For example, Earth's face is alive and shows the Maker through all of its features and orderliness. When Earth dies during winter and is covered with a white shroud, our view of its face is distracted or this wintry corpse of spring diverts our

---

[40] Said Nursi, *The Letters,* vol. 1.

attention to the past and brings a broader spectacle to our eyes.

In other words, all past springs, each a miracle of Divine Power covering Earth's face, urge the conviction that a new spring will come and that Earth's face will be revived and refilled with living creatures. All past springs, as well as Earth's face [which has experienced cycles of life and death for millions of years] bear witness to the necessary Existence, Unity, Permanence, and Eternity of an All-Majestic Maker, an All-Powerful One of Perfection, a Self-Subsistent, Permanent One, so brilliantly and strongly and on such a vast scale, and present such clear proofs, that one cannot help but proclaim: "I believe in God, the One, the Single."

According to the meaning of: *He revives Earth after its death*, just as this lively Earth testifies to the Maker through spring, it also attracts attention to the Divine Power's miracles arranged on the two wings of time—the past and the future—through its death. In place of one spring it shows thousands. It also points to thousands of Power's miracles in place of just one. The testimony of one of those past springs is more decisive than that of the present spring, for all past springs have disappeared, together with their apparent causes, and been replaced by new ones like themselves.

This shows that apparent causes mean nothing, for an All-Powerful One of Majesty creates and dispatches them. However, He makes them dependent on certain causes due to His Wisdom. As for Earth's lively faces, arranged in sequence in time to come, their witness is more forceful, for they will be made while there is yet no sign of them. Each one will be original and, after being sent for definite duties, will be removed.

So, O heedless one drowning in the swamp of naturalism, how can something without a wise and powerful hand reaching all past and future interfere with Earth's living face? Can chance and nature, which mean nothing (with respect to creating, sustaining, and causing to die) have a hand in this? If you want to be freed from this swamp, say: "Nature is no more than a notebook of Divine Power, and chance is the veil of a hidden Divine Wisdom that hides our ignorance," and draw close to the truth.

TWENTY-FIFTH WINDOW: A work of art shows

an artist. Something born requires the existence of something giving birth. Being below implies being above. And so on. Like all relative things or qualities in pairs existing in relation to each other and requiring the existence of each other, the contingency of all that exists, whether the particular or the whole, shows necessity, for it is equally possible for something to exist or not exist. The being or becoming or being acted upon observed throughout the universe show activity. Their being created shows the activity of creating. Their observed multiplicity and composition necessitate unity.

Necessity, acting, doing, creating, and unity demand the attributes of being necessary, active, creative, and one, all of which are not contingent, passive, multiple, composed, and created. Given this, all contingencies, actions, formations, creations, multiplicities, and compositions in the universe testify to a Necessarily Existent One, One doing whatever He wills, the Creator of all things, One and Single.

In short, contingency shows necessity, being or becoming points to the act of doing or making, and multiplicity points to unity. In the same way, being created and provided, as observed in existence, point to the existence of the acts of making, creating, and providing. These, in turn, point to the existence of a Compassionate Maker, Who is the Creator and Provider. This means that each creature, through the tongues of its hundreds of attributes, bears witness to hundreds of the Necessarily Existent Being's Beautiful Names. If this is not admitted, then all such qualities also must be denied.

TWENTY-SIXTH WINDOW[41]: The beauties and comeliness observed in creatures in the universe appear for a fixed period and then are renewed and refreshed after they disappear. This shows that they are reflections of an Eternal Beauty's manifestations. Just as sparkling troops of bubbles on a river's surface show that the bubbles are mirrors of a perpetual sun's rays, the rays of beauty glittering on creatures traveling in the flowing river of time point to and are the signs of a Permanent Beauty.

The earnest love inherent in the universe's heart also shows a Never-Ending Beloved One. As something that does not exist in a tree's nature

---

[41] This Window concerns people of heart and love.

has no place in its fruits, the solemn, transcendent love existing in humanity, the Tree of Creation's most sensitive and delicate fruit, shows that the universe contains true love, though in different forms and of different kinds. Such a true love in the universe's heart shows an Eternal, Beloved One.

The attractiveness, attractions, and attachments manifesting themselves in the universe's bosom show all alert and aware hearts that they issue from the attractiveness of an attractive, eternal truth. In addition, saintly people and those who can unveil hidden truths in creation, who form the most sensitive and enlightened group of beings, unanimously report that they receive an All-Beautiful One of Majesty's manifestations and are aware, through their illuminations and visions, that the Majestic Beautiful One makes Himself known and loved. This testifies to the existence of a Necessarily Existent One, a Beautiful One of Majesty, and to His making Himself known by human beings. Also, the pen of beautification and decoration shows the beauty of the Names of that pen's Owner by working on the face of the universe and creatures.

Thus the universe, through the beauty on its face, the love in its heart, the attraction in its bosom, the illumination and vision in its eyes, and its pervasive decoration and loveliness, opens a pleasant, clear window. To intellects and hearts, and to those who are alert and awake, it displays a Beautiful One of Majesty, a Never-Ending Beloved One, an Eternal Object of Worship—all of Whose Names are Beautiful.

So, O heedless one struggling in the darkness of materialism and illusions, in suffocating doubts and conjectures, come to your senses! Ascend in a way befitting humanity and look through these openings. See the grace and beauty of Oneness, obtain perfect belief, and be a true human being.

TWENTY-SEVENTH WINDOW: Consider the following verse:

> God is the Creator of all things, and He
> is a Guardian, a Watcher over all things.
> (39:62)

Looking at visible things as well as causes and effects in the universe, we see that the greatest cause—by itself—cannot cause even the most insignificant thing to exist. Thus causes are only a veil, for there must be one who brings effects (things) into existence. Out of innumerable creatures, consider the human faculty of memory, located in a mustard-seed-sized place in a person's head. Despite its tiny size, it is so comprehensive that it contains a book, or rather a library, in which his or her entire life-history is recorded.

What cause can you present as the origin of that miracle of Divine Power? The brain's entangled nerves? The cell's simple, unconscious parts? The winds of chance? In reality, that miracle of art is the work of such a One, a Wise Maker. To remind us in the Hereafter's Supreme Plain of Gathering of what we did in this world, He copies our deeds' register and gives it to our intellect as memory.

Compare all eggs, seeds, and fruit pits to our memory, and then compare all other effects to these tiny miracles of Power. Whatever effect or thing you look at, you will see that it contains such a wonderful artistry that if not only its own cause but all causes were gathered together, they would display their impotence in front of it. For example, some people describe the sun as a huge cause or agent. Supposing it were conscious and had willpower, if you asked it to make a fly's body, it obviously would answer: "Thanks to my Creator's grace, my shop contains a great deal of light and heat and several colors. However, a fly's body contains eyes, ears, life, and other things that are not in my shop or within my capacity."

A thing's amazing art and decoration refute causes (as accounting for its creation) and point to the Necessarily Existent Being, the Producer of All Causes—according to the meaning of: *Unto Him is returned the whole of the affair* (11:123)—and acknowledge Him as the true originator of all things and events. Similarly the results, purposes, and benefits connected to things show that they are products (of the acts) of an All-Munificent Lord, a Compassionate Wise One acting behind the veil of causes.

Since unconscious causes cannot pursue a purpose, how can we explain the fact that every creature comes into existence for many definite purposes and benefits, and according to many instances of wisdom? The only answer is that an All-Wise and All-Munificent Lord brings them into existence, and makes those benefits the reason for their existence.

Consider the coming of rain. Rain's apparent causes have no consideration or concern for animals. Therefore it is sent to help animals through the Wisdom of a Compassionate Creator Who creates and then provides for them. Rain is called a "mercy," for it bears many results of mercy and brings many benefits. It is as if mercy is embodied in raindrops and falls in drops.

The show and embellishment in all adorned plants and animals, which smile at all creatures, also point to a Majestic Being's necessary Existence and Unity and to the One Who, behind the veil of the Unseen, wills to make Himself known and loved through that adornment and embellishment. All of this points to the qualities of making oneself known and loved, which, in turn, testify to the necessary Existence and Unity of a Known, All-Loving, and All-Powerful Maker.

In short, causes are infinitely ordinary and impotent when compared to effects (things), which are full of art and valuable. So how can they have any real part in creation? Also, the benefits of things and the purposes pursued through and for them deny causes any real role in creation, for they attribute their existence to an All-

Wise Maker. Moreover, their decorations and the skills apparent in their coming into existence point to an All-Wise Maker Who wills to make His Power known to conscious beings, Who wills to be loved.

O helpless one who deifies causes! How do you explain these important realities? Why do you deceive yourself? If you are rational, tear the veil of causes apart and, proclaiming: "He is One, without partner," be saved from innumerable illusions.

TWENTY-EIGHTH WINDOW: Consider the following verse:

> Among His signs are His creation of the heavens and Earth and the difference of your tongues and colors. Surely in this are signs for those who know. (30:22)

We see an all-inclusive wisdom and ordering in the universe, from a body's cells to the world. When looking at a body's cells, we see a significant organization and arrangement by the command and law of the One Who sees and governs all bodily functions and needs. The body stores nourishment as fat to be used when needed, and cells also have this ability to store. We see a wise organization, cultivation, and nursery in plants; a generous subsistence and breeding in animals; a majestic management and illumination in the universe's pillar-like parts, each of which serves important purposes; and a perfectly planned and ordered world for certain sublime instances of wisdom and exalted purposes.

As explained and argued in the First Station of The Twenty-second Word, these facts make it impossible to associate any partner with God. From the tiniest particle to the largest star, everything is intertwined and interrelated in such a way that one who does not subjugate and manage stars cannot dominate a particle. Also, as explained and argued in the Second Station of The Twenty-second Word, one who cannot create the heavens and put them in an exact order cannot give anyone a unique face.

All of this forms a window as large as the universe so that, if we look through it, both the person's and the mind's eye see clearly that the meaning of: *God is the Creator of all things and He is a Guardian, a Watcher, over all things. His are the keys of the heavens and Earth...* (39:62-63) are inscribed on the pages of the universe in capital letters. Those who do not see them have no eyes or heart, or only appear to be human.

TWENTY-NINTH WINDOW: Consider the following verse:

> There is nothing that does not glorify Him with praise. (17:44)

Once during spring, I was traveling amid thoughts and feelings of loneliness. At a hill's base, I saw a yellow wild flower that reminded me of similar flowers I had seen in the past in my hometown and other places. It then struck me whose stamp that flower bore, whose seal and inscription it carried. I realized with certainty that all similar flowers on Earth's face were His stamps and seals.

This thought led to the idea that just as a letter's seal announces the one who wrote and sent it, so is that flower a seal of the All-Merciful One. Both that flower and hill, which have been worked with such inscriptions and "lines" of meaningful plants, are letters of that flower's Maker. The hill is a seal, and the plain ahead of it is a letter of the All-Merciful One.

These thoughts led to the following truth: Each thing, being like a seal of the Lord, attributes all things to its Creator and proves that it is a letter of its Author. Thus each thing forms such a window on Divine Unity that it submits all things to a Single One of Unity's ownership. This is especially true of living things, each of which contains such a wonderful design and miraculous art that the One Who makes it so and designs it so meaningfully is also the One Who makes all things. Given this, that one must be He Who has made all things. One who cannot make everything cannot create one thing.

O you who are unaware of the reality of things, look at the universe's face! Can you deny the testimony of the pages of creatures, all of which are like innumerable letters of the Eternally-Besought-of-All, one within the other? Can you deny that the seals put on them are the seals of Divine Unity? How can you silence them? If you listen to any of them with your heart, you will hear it say: "I bear witness that there is no god but God."

THIRTIETH WINDOW: Consider these verses:

> Had there been gods in either (the heavens and Earth) besides God, both would surely be in disorder. (21:22)

> All things perish except His Face. His is the absolute dominion, and unto Him you are returning. (28:88)

This window is for theologians who base their arguments on the facts that all things are contingent (not absolutely necessary) and have come into existence over time. They follow this way in proving the Necessarily Existent One's Existence. Referring their explanations to such voluminous scholarly books as *Sharh al-Mawaqif* and *Sharh al-Maqasid*, we will try to reflect a few rays coming to the soul from the light of the Qur'an through that window, as follows:

Authority and sovereignty do not allow rivalry, partnership, or interference. If a village had two leaders, its order and peace would be destroyed. A district or town with two governors would experience great confusion, and a country with two kings (or governments) would be in constant turmoil. Since this pale shadow of absolute authority and sovereignty enjoyed by powerless people who are not self-sufficient rejects rivalry and the intervention of its opposite, consider how strongly true sovereignty, in the form of supreme, absolute kingdom and authority at the degree of Divine Lordship enjoyed by an Absolutely Powerful One, rejects interference and partnership. In other words, Oneness and Singleness without partners is the most indispensable and constant requirement of Divinity and Lordship.

The universe's perfect order and most beautiful harmony testify to this. The universe has such a perfect order from a fly's wing to the heavens' lamps that our minds cannot comprehend it fully. All we can do is express our amazement and admiration by saying: "Glory be to God. What wonders He has willed. God bless it," and prostrate.

If there were any room for associating partners with God to interfere with Him, according to the meaning of: *Had there been gods in either besides God, both would surely be in disorder* (21:22), order would be destroyed and the universe's form and shape would change. But, as stated in: *Turn your sight (to the heavens) whether you can see any flaw and fissure. Turn again your sight a second time so that your sight will return to you dimmed and dazzled, in a state worn out* (67:3-4), however hard we look for a flaw in creation, our gaze will return exhausted and inform our fault-finding reason: "I have exhausted myself in vain, for there is no flaw." This shows that the order is perfect, which means that this perfect order testifies to God's Oneness.

Creation Indicates God's Existence and Unity

Given that the universe came into existence at a point in time and so is not eternal, theologians argue:

> The world is subject to change. Anything subject to change has a beginning, for it came into existence at a point in time. Anything that came into existence at a point in time has someone who brought it into existence. That being the reality, this universe has an Eternal Creator.

We say:

> The universe certainly has a beginning, for it came into existence at a point in time. We see one world replaced by a new one every century, every year, even every season. Thus there is an All-Powerful One of Majesty Who invents and creates a new world every year, every season, or even every day.
>
> After showing it to conscious beings, He replaces it with a newer one. He makes these worlds succeed each other, attaching them to the string of time in a series. The Power of an All-Powerful One creates this series of renewed worlds in this way. The One Who does this obviously created the universe. He has made this universe and Earth a guest-house for those mighty guests.

As for contingency, theologians argue:

> Contingency means equality between two possibilities. That is, if it is equally possible for something to come into existence or not, there must be one to prefer either possibility, one to create according to this preference, for contingent beings cannot create each other one after the other. Nor can they go back to eternity in cycles with the former having created the latter. Given this, there is a Necessarily Existent Being Who creates all.
>
> Theologians have disproved the chain of creative cause and effect, as well as the notion of successive creators, with 12 decisive arguments, some of which they call "argument in ascension" and "argument in steps." Breaking the chain of cause and effect, they have proved the Necessarily Existent Being's Existence.

We say:

> Rather than showing the impossibility of the chain of cause and effect in creation or the cycle of successive creators to prove the necessary Existence of a Creator Who has no beginning and has created all things, it is better and easier to show the stamp on everything belonging to the Creator of all things. Through the Qur'an's enlightenment, all Windows

> and Words follow this principle. The subject of contingency embraces a broad range of arguments to display the Necessarily Existent Being's Existence in innumerable ways.

However, the subject does not need to be restricted to the way theologians treat it, namely, that the cycle or chain of cause and effect must stop at the point where the realm of Divine Creativity must begin. Rather, it opens up innumerable ways to knowledge of the Necessarily Existent Being.

For example, each thing hesitates when faced with the many possibilities it could choose concerning its being, features, qualities, and lifespan. But we see that it chooses a well-ordered, well-established way so that it acquires the most appropriate body, and that it is equipped with the qualities necessary for its existence, as well as for all the state, conditions, and features it will experience during its life. This is through the will of One Who assigns to everything its specialties, through the choice of One Who chooses, and through the creation of a wise Creator Who directs it for wise purposes along its unique way.

He then clothes it with befitting features and qualities and makes it a part of a composite entity, which only increases the possibilities before it, for it is equally possible for it to have a place in that entity in thousands of ways. However, it is positioned in the most appropriate way so that it can perform the fruitful and purposeful duties expected of it.

The entity then becomes part of a larger entity, which multiplies possibilities still further. Just like before, it is positioned so that it can carry out its important duties. This accurately and decisively demonstrates an All-Wise Director's necessary Existence and shows that things are directed through an All-Knowing Authority's command.

A private has certain duties and specially determined services to perform in relation to his squad, company, battalion, regiment, corps and army, and wisely arranged relations specific to each. Likewise, a cell in your eye's pupil has a certain relation to your eye and then to your head, veins, nervous system, and body as a whole. It also has duties apportioned to it wisely in relation to each. If it did not perform its least duty, you would become ill and the body would suffer.

Just as each creature proclaims a Necessarily Existent One via its being, features, body, form, and attributes, each one also proclaims its Maker in other tongues when positioned in different composite entities. With respect to its services and duties in each entity, it bears witness to the All-Wise Maker's necessary Existence, Will, and Choice. Only the Creator of composite entities, Who positions a thing in such a way that the wise relations between them are maintained, can do such things. This means that one thing has one position where it will testify to Him in thousands of tongues.

As a result, such testimonies of the Necessarily Existent Being's Existence far surpass the number of the creatures in the universe. In fact, they reach the number of possible qualities, features, forms, positions, and duties assigned to each, as well as the relations they maintain in the composite entities in which they are located. So, you who are unaware, just how deaf do you have to be not to hear this testimony filling the universe? What do you say?

THIRTY-FIRST WINDOW: Consider the following verses:

> We have created humanity in the fairest creation and in the best pattern. (95:4)

> In Earth are signs for the people of certainty, and in your selves. Will you still not have insight? (51:20-21)

This window discusses humanity and a person's inner world. As detailed explanations are available in many scholarly books, we will mention only a few fundamentals we have obtained from the Qur'an's enlightenment. As explained in The Eleventh Word and others, each person is such a comprehensive copy (of existence) that Almighty God makes all of His Names perceived by the individual through his or her self. Here we discuss only the following three points:

FIRST POINT: Human beings are mirrors to the Divine Names in three aspects:

First aspect: Just as the night's darkness suggests light, all people point, through their weakness and impotence, destitution and neediness, imperfection and defects, to an All-Powerful One of Majesty's Power, Force, Wealth, Mercy, and so on. Thus each person becomes a mirror to many of God's Attributes. Searching for a point of support against countless obstacles and enemies in our infinite weakness and impotence, our conscience is always turned toward the Necessarily Existent Being.

Our infinite destitution and neediness compel us to look for a point of assistance in order to realize our innumerable aims, and so our conscience always tends to receive support from the Court of a Compassionate, Wealthy One, and we petition Him for our needs. Thus, with respect to our need for a point of support and of assistance, two small windows open from each person's conscience onto a Compassionate All-Powerful One's Court of Mercy, through which we can look to Him.

Second aspect: Each of us has a specific God-given knowledge, power, sight, hearing, ownership, and sovereignty. As a result, we function as a mirror to the (Attributes of) Absolute Knowledge, Power, Sight, Hearing, and Ownership of the universe's Owner and His Lordship's sovereignty. Each person understands them and makes them known. For example: "I built this house and know how to build it. I own, see, and administer it. So this huge palace of the universe must have a builder who knows, sees, and administers it."

Third aspect: Each person functions as a mirror to the Divine Names inscribed upon him or her. As stated at the beginning of the Third Station of The Thirty-second Word, the inscriptions of more than 70 Divine Names are apparent in our comprehensive nature. For example, we build something and thereby manifest the Names the Maker, Creator, and Giver of Form. By being the best pattern and the fairest creation, we demonstrate the Names the Most Merciful and Most Compassionate. Our good sustenance and upbringing display the Names the All-Munificent and All-Gracious. All our bodily systems and parts, members and organs, faculties and features, and senses and feelings display different inscriptions of different Divine Names. Just as there is the Greatest Name among the Divine Names, the greatest among the inscriptions of the Names is humanity.

If you know you are human, read yourself or you may remain human only in appearance.

SECOND POINT: This relates to a significant mystery of God's Oneness: Each person's spirit has a unifying function in regard to his or her body, for it causes all bodily members and parts to help each other. In other words, the spirit, a conscious law of Divine Command issuing from Divine Will and a faculty breathed into each of us by God and clothed in a perceptible existence, is not confused by the signals coming from all bodily elements. Rather, the spirit meets all of their needs simultaneously. Distance or nearness are irrelevant, and bodily organs do not prevent each other from communicating with it.

When necessary, the spirit can send most bodily elements to help a single one or move all bodily parts at once. It also can know, perceive, and govern through any of them. If it has refined and purified itself, thereby acquiring sufficient luminosity, it can see and hear through any bodily part.

Seeing that the spirit, a law of Divine Command,[42] displays such abilities in our bodies, the Necessarily Existent Being cannot be confused by countless actions, sounds and voices, invocations and deeds. His universal Will and absolute Power deal with all of them at once and without confusion, for the Majestic Creator sees all things and hears all sounds and voices. As distance has no meaning for Him, He can send, if He wills, all things to help one thing.

---

[42] The spirit has the same meaning for the body as, for example, the law of growth has for a tree. However, the spirit, in contrast to all Divine Laws related to the universe's creation and operation, is alive, conscious, and has a perceptible existence.

THIRD POINT: Life has a significant nature and an important duty. Since this has been detailed in the Twenty-third Window as well as The Twentieth Letter's Eighth Phrase, we recall here only the following point: The complex and complicated senses, feelings and sentiments boiling in life point to many of God's Names and Attributes. They function as clear mirrors to the Ever-Living, Self-Subsistent One's essential Qualities and acts. Since it is not appropriate to discuss this matter before those who deny God and belief in Him, we stop here.

THIRTY-SECOND WINDOW: Consider the following verses:

> He sent His Messenger with guidance and the true religion in order to make it triumphant over all other religions. God is sufficient as a witness. (48:28)

> Say: "O humanity! I am the Messenger of God to you all, for Whom is the absolute dominion of the heavens and Earth; there is no god but He. He gives life and causes to die." (7:158)

This window is formed of Prophet Muhammad, the sun of the heaven of Messengership. Having explained this in great detail in the

Nineteenth and Thirty-first Words, as well as The Nineteenth Letter,[43] we discuss only this point:

On the wings of Messengership and sainthood, that is, equipped with a power formed of the absolute consensus of all Prophets preceding him and the unanimous agreement of all saints and pure scholars to come after him, Prophet Muhammad, himself an articulate proof of Divine Unity, proclaimed and demonstrated Divine Unity throughout his life with all his strength. He opened up onto knowledge of God a broad and radiant window, namely the Muslim world.

Thousands of pure, truth-seeking and truthful scholars like Imam Ghazzali, Imam Rabbani, Muhiy al-Din ibn al-'Arabi, and 'Abd al-Qadir al-Jilani look through this window and point others to knowledge of God. Is there a veil to draw across such a window? Can one who criticizes this window and does not look through it be considered sensible? You give the answer.

THIRTY-THIRD WINDOW: Consider these verses:

> All praise be to God, Who has sent down to His servant the Book and has allowed therein no crookedness. (18:1)

---

[43] Said Nursi, *The Letters*, (The Light, 2002).

> *Alif Lam Mim Ra.* A Book which We
> have sent to you so that you may bring
> men forth from darkness to light. (14:1)

Consider these Windows as a few drops from the Qur'an's ocean and try to understand how many lights of Divine Unity, like water of life, there are in the Qur'an. Even if you have a simple, superficial look at the Qur'an, the source and mine of all previous Windows, still it is a most shining, luminous, comprehensive Window.

To understand how brilliant and luminous that Window is, you may refer to the Treatise of the Qur'an's Miraculousness, which is the Twenty-fifth Word and the Eighteenth Sign of the Nineteenth Letter. Supplicating the Throne of Mercy of the Majestic Being, Who sent us the Qur'an, we say:

> Our Lord! Do not call us to account if we
> have forgotten or made errors! Our Lord!
> Do not cause our hearts to swerve after
> You have guided us! Our Lord! Accept
> from us, surely You are the All-Hearing,
> the All-Knowing. Accept our penitence,
> surely You are the Oft-Relenting, the All-
> Merciful.

A note

I hope this Thirty-third Word with 33 windows may help an unbeliever to accept belief, may strengthen the belief of one whose belief is weak, and lead one with strong belief based on imitation to have substantial belief, and then to expand that substantial belief. I hope it may lead one with expanded belief to progress in knowledge of God, which is the source of all kinds of true progress and evolution, and open up before him more luminous, more brilliant scenes. For this reason, you should regard one window to be enough for you, for even if your mind has received its share and obtained conviction, your heart will also demand its share, as will your spirit. Even the imaginative faculty will demand its share from that light. It is because of this that each window has benefits of its own.

> Peace be upon those who follow the true guidance. May those who follow their whims and illusions receive what they deserve. Glory be to You. We have no knowledge save what You have taught us. You are All-Knowing, All-Wise. O God, bestow blessings and peace upon him whom You sent as a mercy for the worlds, and upon his Family and Companions. Amen.

Index

A

Adam (Prophet), 59, 185
angels, 28, 58, 82, 85, 90, 105, 113, 126, 132, 138, 176, 193
animals, 6, 7, 10, 11, 22, 49, 50, 72, 75, 97, 105, 132, 133, 140, 147, 162, 176, 185, 188, 190, 195, 210, 236, 237
Arabic, 2, 22, 27, 209
atom, 36, 37, 39, 40, 42, 43, 66, 68, 69, 70, 75, 77, 92, 94

B

balance, 34, 82, 88, 163, 206, 212, 218
Beauty (Divine), 45, 55, 56, 103, 117, 118, 119, 123, 127, 134, 137, 138, 150, 174, 176, 177, 207, 231
belief, 25, 26, 27, 57, 59, 61, 98, 106, 109, 117, 129, 145, 147, 149, 152, 164, 176, 197, 233, 252, 255
Book of the Universe, 8, 42, 44, 47, 54, 57, 89, 93

C

carnal self, 144, 148, 150, 153, 157, 158, 163, 164
causality, 42, 69, 76, 78, 80, 96, 143, 145
cause, 3, 18, 29, 64, 83, 84, 86, 91, 96, 97, 105, 107, 117, 132, 135, 141, 148, 152, 154, 157, 173, 174, 175, 204, 205, 206, 218, 222, 233, 234, 244, 245, 254
cause and effect, 29, 96, 244, 245
chance, 3, 6, 8, 10, 68, 83, 141, 142, 196, 204, 207, 215, 218, 220, 222, 229, 234
Christians, 164
civilization, 88, 139, 143, 145, 149
Companions, 56, 64, 84, 129, 164, 177, 255
compassion, 12, 105, 117, 123, 132, 135, 147, 154, 155, 162, 163, 165, 172, 183, 195, 203

conscience, 61, 120, 248
consciousness, 4, 37, 40, 48, 97, 100, 200
contentment, 153
contingency, 230, 244, 245
contingent, 104, 204, 230, 241, 244
creation, 5, 8, 46, 48, 51, 55, 57, 59, 62, 66, 72, 73, 76, 82, 83, 85, 86, 88, 90, 91, 92, 94, 96, 97, 103, 106, 107, 109, 115, 117, 124, 125, 127, 128, 130, 134, 136, 151, 170, 182, 185, 187, 191, 196, 197, 202, 232, 235, 236, 237, 242, 244, 245, 247, 250, 251

D

death, 30, 31, 32, 45, 53, 54, 84, 122, 141, 143, 145, 146, 155, 166, 167, 187, 221, 223, 227, 228
desire, 128, 132, 147, 165, 177, 197
despair, 98, 155, 159, 166
Destiny, 8, 38, 43, 75, 76, 106, 155, 182
destruction, 76, 107, 151, 226
disease, 72
disobedience, 172
dissipation, 143, 168
diversity, 74, 77, 205

E

enjoyment, 3, 124, 125, 141, 148, 169
enlightenment, 25, 174, 244, 248
eternal life, 147, 156, 176
eternity, 46, 54, 76, 77, 149, 179, 244
ether, 99
evil, 128, 150, 168
evolution, 143, 255
Existence (Divine), 1, 26, 32, 37, 40, 54, 58, 89, 90, 92, 103, 180, 182, 183, 184, 186, 187, 188, 189, 190, 191, 193, 194, 198, 199, 201, 202, 203, 207, 209, 212, 213, 217, 219, 221, 222, 226, 227, 228, 236, 241, 244, 246, 247
extinction, 54, 143, 161, 227

F

falsehood, 62
fear, 141, 142, 146, 167, 179
free will, 97, 141
freedom, 139, 145
future, 21, 39, 74, 76, 228,

229

G

generosity, 123, 204
al-Ghazzali, 253
grace, 25, 48, 82, 121, 122, 126, 127, 133, 135, 136, 137, 148, 150, 155, 159, 164, 188, 195, 202, 203, 207, 211, 212, 215, 224, 233, 235
gratitude, 114, 124, 137, 153, 156, 157, 158, 159, 170, 171
grave, 103, 140, 143, 146, 149, 150, 166, 174
guidance, 25, 61, 62, 252, 255

H

happiness, 61, 123, 124, 125, 132, 139, 144, 145, 150, 151, 165, 166
harmony, 2, 33, 82, 174, 204, 207, 242
heart, 33, 34, 61, 63, 106, 107, 120, 137, 148, 155, 157, 171, 182, 223, 231, 233, 238, 240, 255
heavens, 26, 31, 35, 50, 59, 60, 63, 65, 80, 82, 83, 84, 88, 90, 92, 94, 96, 109, 126, 132, 151, 152, 187, 204, 208, 210, 213, 217, 237, 238, 240, 242, 252
heedlessness, 128, 140, 190, 204, 207, 210
Hell, 83, 140
Hereafter, 105, 126, 128, 129, 139, 149, 150, 163, 164, 169, 171, 174, 175, 177, 234

I

Ibn al-'Arabi, 253
idols, 143
ignorance, 16, 96, 200, 229
imagination, 85, 99, 168, 176
immortal, 172, 173
impotence, 40, 104, 145, 200, 220, 234, 248
ingratitude, 154, 213
insight, 86, 89, 248
intellect, 72, 171, 234
intention, 48, 73, 139

J

Jami, 22
Jesus (Prophet), 164
jinn, 105, 113, 126, 132, 138
Joseph (Prophet), 129, 177
jurisprudence, 109
justice, 126, 161, 162, 212

K

knowledge, 16, 25, 36, 39, 42, 43, 46, 57, 62, 63, 64, 67, 68, 69, 71, 72, 73, 74, 84, 95, 97, 100, 108, 109, 117, 121, 129, 131, 135, 162, 177, 190, 192, 193, 209, 211, 225, 245, 249, 253, 255

L

law, 17, 18, 32, 51, 72, 94, 101, 110, 115, 195, 218, 237, 250, 251

life, 13, 17, 31, 32, 35, 39, 41, 42, 45, 49, 51, 53, 54, 57, 63, 66, 68, 71, 76, 101, 102, 107, 115, 117, 123, 126, 137, 145, 147, 153, 155, 156, 167, 168, 169, 176, 182, 199, 200, 223, 224, 225, 226, 228, 235, 245, 252, 253, 254

light, 11, 13, 19, 20, 23, 25, 28, 34, 37, 38, 42, 53, 60, 61, 68, 72, 82, 89, 90, 99, 100, 101, 103, 110, 112, 117, 121, 138, 147, 190, 195, 199, 203, 206, 214, 215, 217, 223, 224, 226, 235, 241, 248, 254, 255

Lordship (Divine), 28, 29, 34, 48, 50, 51, 57, 59, 60, 66, 81, 88, 89, 93, 95, 98, 115, 169, 180, 186, 187, 188, 189, 190, 192, 193, 194, 202, 203, 207, 211, 213, 220, 226, 241, 249

love, 23, 25, 59, 116, 117, 118, 124, 125, 126, 127, 128, 129, 132, 133, 134, 137, 144, 146, 150, 151, 152, 153, 155, 156, 157, 158, 159, 160, 161, 163, 164, 165, 166, 167, 168, 169, 170, 171, 172, 173, 174, 175, 176, 177, 178, 194, 231, 233

M

materialism, 233

matter, 27, 45, 99, 102, 104, 200, 221, 252

memory, 34, 234

mercy, 19, 47, 48, 59, 64, 79, 117, 123, 127, 134, 141, 147, 150, 177, 188, 195, 202, 203, 206, 211, 212, 224, 225, 236, 255

Messengership, 57, 62, 252, 253

mind, 1, 29, 43, 62, 63, 68, 72, 99, 121, 140, 147,

168, 178, 183, 184, 192, 238, 255
miracle, 4, 81, 90, 105, 212, 224, 228, 234

N

naturalism, 78, 223, 229
nature, 8, 10, 15, 42, 43, 49, 55, 66, 68, 69, 72, 73, 81, 83, 97, 114, 119, 130, 131, 141, 142, 143, 145, 156, 159, 183, 186, 197, 198, 199, 201, 204, 207, 220, 225, 229, 232, 250, 252
necessity, 58, 187, 230
neediness, 248
Nimrod, 40
non-existence, 52, 83, 109, 142, 143, 227

O

obedience, 48, 80, 82, 87, 125, 149, 193, 216
order, 1, 2, 7, 8, 23, 33, 40, 45, 48, 49, 59, 69, 71, 72, 74, 75, 76, 79, 81, 86, 87, 88, 92, 108, 163, 182, 184, 189, 191, 193, 201, 202, 204, 207, 211, 212, 218, 219, 223, 238, 241, 242, 249, 252

P

Paradise, 90, 105, 124, 125, 127, 128, 129, 132, 133, 138, 139, 146, 150, 151, 160, 171, 172, 173, 174, 175, 176, 177
partners, 79, 81, 91, 94, 95, 96, 139, 197, 241, 242
past, 21, 74, 76, 167, 169, 177, 228, 229, 239
patience, 155, 166
penitence, 254
Pharaoh, 40
philosophy, 66, 69, 70, 72, 74, 76, 79, 81, 83, 130, 196
pity, 142, 164
pleasure, 112, 116, 117, 123, 125, 126, 132, 139, 142, 145, 148, 157, 158, 165, 166, 167, 168, 170, 172, 173, 175
poverty, 145, 200
prayer, 23, 183, 185
progress, 42, 143, 149, 255
property, 15, 67
Prophets, 57, 58, 62, 118, 156, 164, 166, 173, 192, 253
punishment, 18, 19, 142, 144, 223

purify, 221
purity, 61, 82, 121
purpose, 83, 87, 114, 131, 181, 203, 235

Q

R

Rabbani, 174, 253
Rafidites, 164
reality, 23, 29, 31, 59, 74, 80, 111, 119, 126, 131, 141, 145, 152, 183, 224, 234, 240, 243
reason, 19, 30, 32, 61, 95, 107, 137, 138, 187, 192, 235, 242, 255
reasoning, 31, 86, 89, 98
rebellion, 168
reflection, 35, 53, 153, 157, 160, 167
religion, 59, 83, 252
renewal, 227
Resurrection, 108, 109, 223
Revelation, 58, 61
reward, 147, 170, 172, 173, 175
Risale-i Nur, 27, 96, 217

S

sainthood, 128, 253
saints, 57, 58, 61, 118, 122, 127, 129, 150, 156, 164, 166, 173, 192, 193, 253
Satan, 139
science, 66, 74, 77, 79, 111, 125, 143
scientism, 196
season, 202, 243
security, 149
self, 145, 147, 165, 248
self-confidence, 139
selfhood, 12, 163, 171
self-sufficient, 241
separation, 44, 112, 140, 143, 145, 146, 157, 163, 166, 205, 206
servanthood, 82
service, 68, 156, 227
Sharh al-Mawaqif, 117, 241
Shari'a, 58, 59
Solomon, 177
soul, 73, 241
spirit, 99, 105, 108, 121, 132, 137, 143, 148, 160, 161, 171, 193, 208, 250, 251, 255
spirit beings, 99, 105, 132, 138, 193
submission, 48, 61, 79, 83, 87, 193

T

technology, 143
theologians, 241, 243, 244, 245
theology, 95
transience, 146, 164, 169
Truth, 60, 85, 161, 162, 178

U

ugliness, 205
unbelief, 21
unity, 15, 19, 51, 54, 230, 231
Unity (Divine), 1, 21, 25, 26, 27, 28, 31, 32, 37, 38, 40, 41, 42, 44, 46, 47, 52, 53, 54, 57, 58, 65, 66, 67, 82, 84, 89, 90, 91, 92, 94, 96, 98, 104, 106, 112, 128, 138, 163, 180, 182, 185, 186, 187, 188, 189, 190, 191, 192, 193, 194, 196, 197, 198, 201, 203, 207, 209, 212, 213, 217, 218, 219, 221, 222, 223, 224, 227, 228, 236, 240, 253, 254

V

vicegerent, 220
virtue, 67, 116, 117, 123

W

weakness, 145, 200, 248
willpower, 96, 142, 146
wisdom, 10, 12, 19, 24, 36, 48, 49, 54, 66, 69, 70, 71, 72, 73, 74, 76, 77, 78, 80, 82, 85, 87, 90, 106, 131, 135, 160, 161, 162, 183, 184, 188, 189, 191, 192, 198, 201, 202, 203, 206, 210, 211, 212, 215, 216, 217, 218, 219, 222, 224, 225, 227, 235, 237
worship, 73, 83, 91, 98, 116, 125, 129, 144, 150, 165, 168, 170, 172, 175, 193, 194, 223

X

Y

Z